D0272472

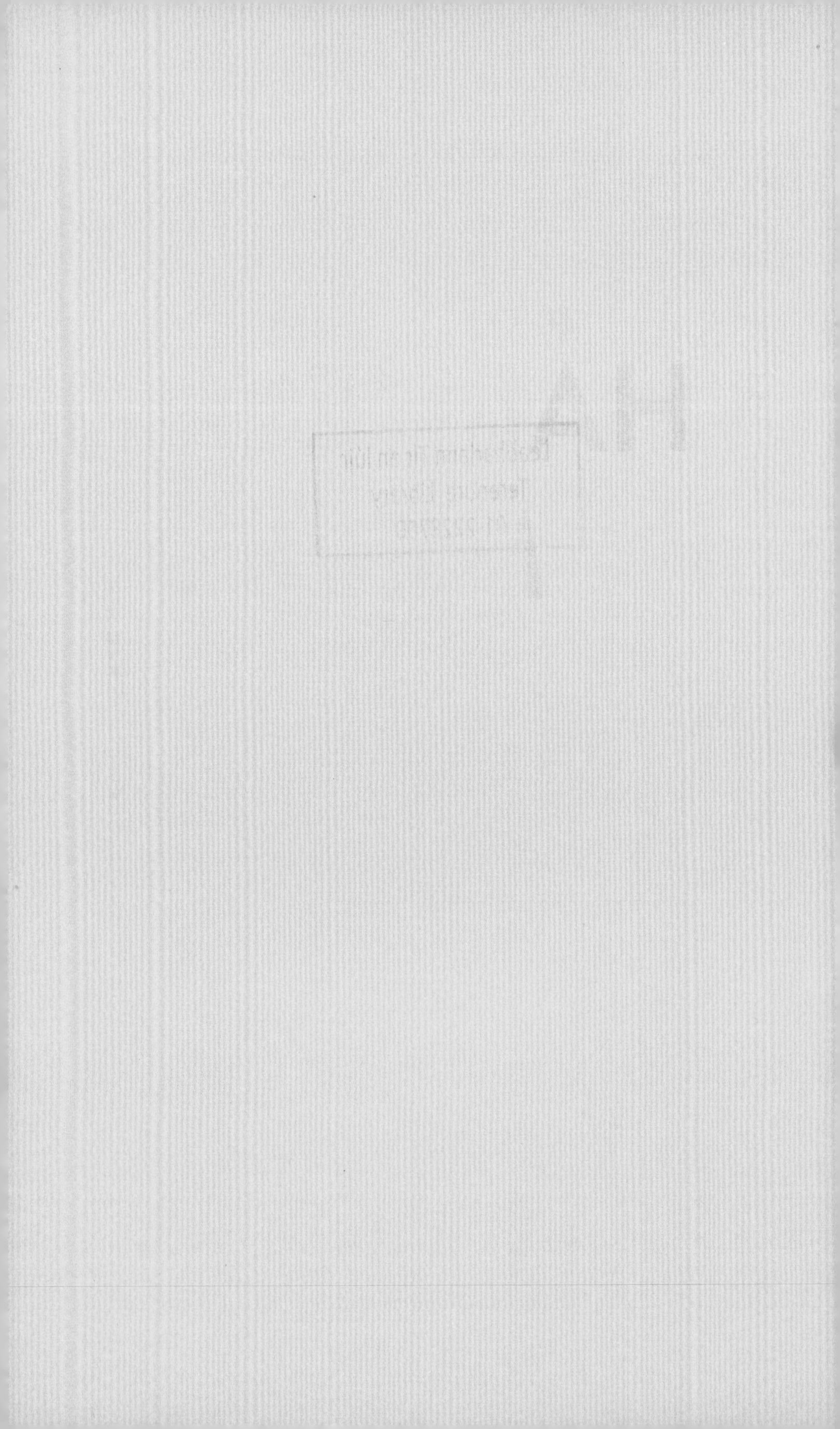

HARVEY *and* ME

KATIE PRICE

HARVEY *and* ME

mB
MIRROR BOOKS

I would like to dedicate this book to my family who have supported me throughout Harvey's journey, and the NHS for providing Harvey with all the care and attention he needs.

And most importantly I'd like to thank my Harvey Price for being my wonderful, bright and intelligent loving son.

MIRROR BOOKS

1

Published in Great Britain and Ireland in 2021 by
Mirror Books, a Reach PLC business,
5 St Paul's Square, Liverpool, L3 9SJ.

www.mirrorbooks.co.uk
@TheMirrorBooks

Hardback ISBN: 9781913406691
eBook ISBN: 9781913406707

Photographic acknowledgements:
Katie Price, Glen Gratton, OK magazine, Alamy.

Design and production by Mirror Books.

Printed and bound by CPI Group (UK) Ltd,
Croydon, CR0 4YY.

CONTENTS

Introduction 1

1. Harvey Daniel Price 5
2. Welcome To The World 25
3. The Day Everything Changed 41
4. Working Mum 60
5. One Of A Kind 70
6. Challenging Behaviour 83
7. Nanny Nightmares 112
8. Father Figures 129
9. Sibling Bond 140
10. Harvey's Law 148
11. Educating Harvey 166
12. Defying The Odds 180
13. On The Right Track 197
14. Amy 204
15. A Grandmother's Love 213
16. Complex Conditions 226
17. Medication 243
18. Suited And Booted 247
19. The Next Chapter 257

With thanks

I would like to thank my mum for always being there to support me and helping in so many ways with this book. And thanks to Georgia Trevitt for working closely with me to write this book and to Mirror Books for having faith in me and allowing me to tell mine and Harvey's story. I hope this book helps the many families and carers out there who have inspired me to keep going and have provided a network of support.

A massive thank you to the charities Mencap and Anna Kennedy Online for the help they provide me and the many families across the UK with. Your help and generosity is always appreciated.

Finally I'd like to say thank you to the general public for supporting my #TrackaTroll campaign. Let's stamp out online abuse for good.

INTRODUCTION

'I love you.'

'I love you too, Harvey.'

'Forever?'

'Forever.'

Who knew three little words could mean so much? I was told my son would never be able to talk, so the fact he can tell me he loves me every single day is a miracle.

Before I had Harvey, I was known as Jordan in the tabloids – apparently a bimbo who was obsessed with fame and loved partying.

There's always been much more to me than that, but having Harvey forced me to grow up very quickly. He's made me a better person. He's taught me to never give up because no matter what has been thrown his way, he has never given up.

I can't imagine a life without Harvey. I truly believe he was sent to me for a reason. I've always had a caring side and wanted to look after someone, so I feel like it was all meant to be. Our bond is unbreakable.

Strip back who I am and what I do for a living, this is me as a mum. I'm sure you've read a lot of stories about me over the years – some true, some couldn't be further from true. But away from the headlines, I'm just someone who wants the best for their children.

So, who is my son Harvey? Harvey is a 6ft, 26 stone 19-year-old with the mental age of around seven years old. He has a long list of complex conditions, including septo-optic dysplasia, autism and Prader-Willi syndrome – just to name a few – which you'll learn more about as you read on.

But that doesn't define him. Harvey is also very caring and kind. He's sweet, funny and unpredictable. He's a strong character who knows what he wants – and he won't stop until he gets it. I have no idea who he takes after…

Throughout his life, he's faced many challenges. He's had diagnosis after diagnosis, but he's defied the odds. He's just started college and I couldn't be prouder of him. He really is one in a million. I'm blessed to have him and I wouldn't change him for the world.

INTRODUCTION

If you follow me on social media, you will have seen his amazing personality. But that's just a snippet of our life. Yes, we have so much fun together, but I don't always show the world the tough times. And trust me, it's tough.

I've brought Harvey up on my own from the very beginning after his dad Dwight Yorke cut contact. I always say that any man can fill a pram, but it takes a real man to be a father.

Despite Harvey's disabilities, I've never had any help. He's my son and I just get on with it. I live and breathe Harvey, so to me, our life is just normal. You have to take every day as it comes. There are good days, and there are bad days. There are funny days, and there are challenging days.

Whatever journey I've been on, Harvey has been with me through everything. He has been the one constant in my life. It's a huge comfort to know that Harvey will always be by my side. My other four children, Junior, Princess, Jett and Bunny, have their dads – and I absolutely hate having to share them.

I wanted to write this book because I feel strongly that Harvey deserves to have his voice heard. It's not just for Harvey, but for every other family out there who are in a similar situation. I want to show that you're not limited just because of your disabilities.

As a parent, you never stop worrying about your

children. But when you have a disabled child, the anxiety is multiplied by a thousand. I've never wanted any credit or sympathy, but I want to try my best to raise awareness and educate people. By sharing our story, I hope to bring love, encouragement and support. From the very beginning, right up until now, we've had tears of sadness, tears of joy, tears of relief, and most importantly, tears of laughter.

So, here goes. This is the story of *Harvey And Me*...

One

HARVEY DANIEL PRICE

'I've just started my career – do I really want a baby?' I thought to myself as I stared at the blue line on the pregnancy test. I was in a relationship with Dwight, but we didn't live together. I was 23 and I would only really see him on weekends. The pregnancy wasn't planned. I wasn't on any type of contraception – and he knew that. But when you're young, you can be a bit naive and careless about it all.

I know it sounds stupid, but I just kind of thought, 'Oh, I won't get pregnant.' But admittedly, I didn't know much about ovulation days back then. I had no idea that there were a certain number of days in a month when you're most likely to get pregnant – your 'fertile window'. Obviously, five kids later, I'm very aware of that now. I've always been extremely fertile – I could probably get pregnant just by looking at a man!

'What am I going to do?' I panicked. My modelling career had just started to really take off. I was in my prime. 'Is this going to ruin my body? Will I still be seen as a sexy pin-up? Am I ever going to be able to work again?' All these thoughts were running through my mind. I love babies so much. I'm very nurturing and I always have been, so I knew I definitely wanted a lot of kids. But I didn't really plan when that would be. I always imagined I would meet someone, fall madly in love, buy a house, get married, have a baby and live happily ever after. I wanted to do it all the traditional way. But wow, my life has been far from traditional.

I told Dwight the news. I had no idea how he was going to react, but it's fair to say it went down like a lead balloon. 'I don't want it,' he said instantly.

There was something inside me telling me I was ready to become a mum, yet I still had a nagging voice in my head that was saying otherwise. It was almost as though I had an angel on one shoulder telling me I'd be brilliant, and a devil on the other giving me conflicting advice.

I was definitely worried about my career, but if I was in a stable relationship, it wouldn't have been such a big dilemma. And my relationship with Dwight was far from stable. After a lot of thinking and toing and froing, I came to the decision that it wasn't right to bring the baby into the world.

Dwight gave me the impression that if I kept it, he wouldn't want to be with me. I didn't think that would be fair on our child. They hadn't even been born yet and they would already be from a broken home. Of course a child doesn't need their dad in their life to flourish, which Harvey is living proof of, but I looked at things very differently back then. Plus, my biological dad, Ray, walked out on the family when I was three and I turned out alright… kind of! That didn't affect me because I had hardly seen him anyway and my stepdad, Paul, took on the father role. I took Paul's last name and I now call him 'Dad'.

I just thought, 'How would I cope on my own?' I was only young and I presumed that nobody would want a single mum. So I booked in to a private clinic to have an abortion. When I told Dwight, he didn't even offer to pay towards it. And at that point in my career, I wasn't loaded like people would probably think. In fact, he didn't offer me any support whatsoever. He didn't even ask if I was okay. Having an abortion wasn't a decision I took lightly – I don't think it is for any woman. So it would have been nice to have him there with me.

I actually ended up going to the abortion clinic a total of three times. The first time, I got to the car park and I was ready to go in, but I pulled out at the very last minute. I actually made it inside the second time. I was sitting in the waiting room and listening for my name to be called out. 'I can't do this,' I thought. So I got up and left.

The third – and final – time, I very nearly went through with it. I just remember sitting in my gown and being shown a scan of the baby on the screen. How wrong is that? I even heard a little heartbeat. I didn't want to be reminded of the life growing inside of me. I just couldn't go through with it. Something was stopping me from going ahead. It was that voice on my shoulder again.

So, instead of being negative and feeling worried about the future, I pulled myself together and thought, 'Fuck this and fuck you, Dwight. It's my body and I'll do what I want.' If he didn't want anything to do with the baby, then that was that. I was sticking to my guns no matter what and I was determined to have this baby. I'd made my decision and there was no going back.

My family were all very supportive of my decision, especially my mum, Amy. Despite their worries about me, not once did my parents ever tell me to have an abortion. I know a lot of girls out there would think that they're sorted for life just because their baby's dad is a footballer, but I'm definitely not that type of girl. That never even crossed my mind. And trust me, if I wanted to bag a footballer, I could. Instead, I've always gone for low-lives with no money who scrounge off me and use my name to be the next Mr Price and think they're famous. Will I ever learn?

I told Dwight I was keeping the baby. Not long after, he was pictured coming out of a nightclub holding hands with the television presenter and model Gabrielle Richens – and it was splashed all over a newspaper. At this point, we were still together and I was so humiliated. But when I look back now that I'm older and wiser, I realise how much of a mug I must have looked. It was a blessing in disguise. By outing Dwight, the press had actually done me a massive favour – for once!

Funnily enough, I actually did a photoshoot for the cover of *Loaded Magazine* with Gabby, so she definitely would have known I was with Dwight. They're both as bad as each other. I think they dated for a bit, but obviously that didn't work out, which isn't surprising because anything with a hole was a goal for Dwight. He always found it hard to stay faithful.

I confronted him about Gabby and asked him if he was cheating on me. He denied it of course, but that was it – I was done with him. I must have been a fool not to have noticed he was doing the dirty on me from the very beginning. I used to see hair bands in the bathroom and there'd be glasses with lipstick stains on them. But when I questioned it, he'd just say that he'd had a party and at that time, I didn't think anything of it. Ignorance is bliss, eh?!

I knew I was going to be a single mum from that point on. It was weird to think I had this human being growing inside me and I was creating a little famous baby whose dad was a popular footballer for Manchester United. We may not have been together, but I never thought in a million years that a so-called religious family man wouldn't want to see his own son.

I wanted to make sure that I was making an effort to involve Dwight, so every time I had a scan I'd invite him along. He never took me up on my invitations, so instead, I'd send him pictures of the scans. My mum would always let his manager know as well – and my mum is still in contact with his manager to this day.

I still remember going for my 12-week scan. I felt very alone as all the other women had their partners by their side. Even though I didn't want to be in a relationship with Dwight, it would have been nice to have him there. But as soon as I saw my baby on the screen, nothing else mattered. Seeing the little arms and legs moving around was the most amazing feeling.

I phoned Dwight to tell him that everything was fine and the baby was healthy, but he didn't seem to care. I also bought a baby book from Mothercare to document the pregnancy for Dwight so that he could see all the different stages if he ever wanted to. It was full of photos and notes about each week of the pregnancy. I had even highlighted a part in the book which said that babies can hear their mother and father's voices at the 18-week stage. Subtle, much? But he still didn't take the hint.

When my mum was pregnant with my younger sister Sophie, I remember looking at her book and being fascinated with how a baby grows in the belly. And there I was at 23, buying my very own book with a baby growing in my belly. I bought a book for all of my pregnancies because I think most mums would agree that it's a nice thing to be able to read back. Even now, I sometimes get Harvey's book out and have a flick through.

I can't say I didn't try with Dwight. It wasn't for my sake, but for our baby's sake. I just never, ever wanted my child to say to me, 'You didn't let my dad get involved.' I know I've done right on my side. People forget that as kids grow up, they become curious. They have questions and they want to know the answers. It's like when children who have been adopted go searching for their birth parents when they're older.

I always say to anyone out there, whether you break up with someone or not, don't take it out on the kids because they will always ask questions and you don't want them to take sides. It doesn't matter how much you hate that person, you've got to do right by your child. And it doesn't matter how vile that person has been to you or what the circumstances are, it doesn't mean to say they'd be like that with the kids. I mean look at me, I was married to a serial cheater – my third husband Kieran Hayler – who betrayed me in every single way. But I can't deny the fact he's a good dad to our children Jett and Bunny.

While I was pregnant, I was living with my then best friend Sally in Ruislip, West London. She originally started off as my make-up artist, but we became joined at the hip and we ended up moving in together. We lived together for about five years and we had such a laugh.

We're so chalk and cheese. I miss her a lot. I used to lead her astray – it was never the other way round. I'd be like, 'Shall we go out tonight?' She'd say, 'No, let's just stay in and watch TV.' And then I'd always manage to drag her out with me. 'I'm only having one drink,' she'd insist – and then we'd stumble home ten drinks later.

The reason our friendship was affected was because of an ex-manager of mine. To cut a long story short, Sally was getting married and she asked me to do a speech at her wedding. But my manager at the time warned me against it, as she told me she was just using me for a spread in *OK! Magazine*. During my career, I've believed a lot of people who I perhaps shouldn't have. Of course no one can force me to do something I don't want to do.

I'm my own person. But people definitely put thoughts in my head and I've made some wrong decisions that I now regret. It's fair to say losing my friendship with Sally was a big regret.

We were such great friends and I shouldn't have let something stupid like that come between us. But I've actually been in contact with her since and we've planned to meet up. The funny thing is, all these years later, Sally's mobile number is the only one I know off the top of my head. So if I ever got kidnapped or lost, I'd have to rely on Sally to pick up! I don't even know my own number. But then again, I have changed it loads over the years because dickheads manage to get hold of it.

Anyway, I was in the middle of buying my own house. It was my second house and I was doing it up for me and the baby. I actually bought it before I knew I was pregnant, so the fact I'd decided to buy a three-bedroom house felt like fate because I'd been questioning whether it would be too big for just me.

I desperately wanted to know what I was having, so I found out the sex. One, because I couldn't stand the thought of the doctor knowing while I didn't, and two, because I wanted to decorate the nursery. Which really, in hindsight, didn't actually make any reference to the baby's sex whatsoever because my whole house was cream anyway! I can still picture his room now – I had it painted neutral colours and there was a picture of a big teddy bear on the wall.

I was over the moon to be having a little boy. I told Dwight, thinking it may change things. But no, he still had no interest. Stupidly, I thought he might come to his senses and say that he'd support me. I didn't just need support physically, but emotionally, too.

As a young, single woman, I was still going out with my friends while I was pregnant. But it's not like I was going out and getting pissed. I was driving! The press used to get pictures of me coming out of a club and the shot they used would always be when I'm half-blinking to make it look like I was drunk. Of course they'd never write in the articles that I was driving home afterwards, completely sober.

They'd also make digs about what I was wearing. But bloody hell, when I look back at some of the outfits I wore when I was pregnant, I don't blame them. What was I thinking?! The thing is, I tried to dress sexy because I still had my modelling career. I was still doing shoots while I was pregnant, believe it or not. Some of them were before I'd even told anyone I was pregnant. So I'd be posing in a thong, breathing in as hard as I could and trying my best to look all sexy.

I should have thought, 'Kate, put it away. You're pregnant – no one wants you.' But then again, hello

Gareth Gates! He wanted a bit of the Pricey – even when I was six months pregnant. He denied losing his virginity to me at first, but once he finally admitted it, wasn't that when his career started? Anyway, moving swiftly on…

All these stories would come out about me, saying I was partying until 3am in the morning while I was pregnant. At the end of the day, I was pregnant, I wasn't ill. You don't have to stay in bed all the time just because you're having a baby. I was single and having fun with my friends. I had morning sickness for the first few months, but apart from that, it was a perfect pregnancy. It couldn't have gone any better and I felt great. I did everything by the book as well. Any foods they tell you to avoid, I avoided. And obviously I didn't drink alcohol or smoke once.

My due date soon came around, but nothing was happening. I was absolutely massive by this point! My belly looked like I was about to pop. I was feeling a mixture of nerves and excitement, but I was definitely ready. A very long 12 days went by and he was still inside me, so they decided to induce me. I was booked to go to the hospital at 8am on 26 May.

I was so nervous the night before. I was with Sally, my mum, my manager at the time, Dave Read, and the film crew for my BBC reality show, *Katie Price: The Jordan Years,* including the producer Richard Macer. I used to call him 'Tricky Dicky'. I did love working with him, but I doubt he'd say the same for me. Looking back, I must have been a bloody nightmare for him. Sorry, Richard!

I didn't feel very prepared for the birth. I had no antenatal care and I just kind of went into it all head first. I didn't do any antenatal classes because I just thought you had to be with someone – and obviously I was single. I didn't want to go on my own and I didn't really want to take anyone else because I thought it would be weird. Sally had offered to come with me a few times, but it didn't feel right.

So I went in there not knowing much about what was going to happen. But one thing I will say is that I had a very organised baby bag. It was a yellow bag which my mum used when she had my sister and she passed it down to me. It was full of everything you'd need.

I also bought loads of sleepsuits. His drawers were jam-packed with them before he'd even arrived. I kept getting them out and holding them up in front of me, thinking, 'Oh my God. I can't wait to have this baby.' It made it all feel very real. I think that's the only time in my life I've ever been organised!

Me and my mum also went to Mamas & Papas and bought a new buggy and loads of blankets. Again, the colour scheme I went for was boring. Everything was neutral and cream because I kept visualising what would suit the baby. I used to look at baby magazines and see what colours would suit other mixed-race babies. I thought he'd look gorgeous in cream.

I planned in my head that I would play music while I was giving birth. God knows where I got that idea from! I made a CD full of all my favourite songs and brought it along with me to the hospital.

I also brought a pack of playing cards for us all to play. Do you see what I mean about going into it all head first? I really had no idea about childbirth. In the end, I didn't put the music on once and we didn't play cards. In fact, it was quite the opposite. I just wanted absolute silence. It was so quiet that even the noise of my mum and Sally breathing started to annoy me.

I had Harvey at the Royal Sussex County Hospital, which let's just say was a bit different to The Portland, where I had Junior and Princess! After that, I had Jett in France and I had Bunny at an NHS hospital in Chichester, West Sussex. That was an amazing experience.

The NHS has been incredible many times throughout my life, and that was definitely one of those times. Bunny was six weeks premature and had to spend three weeks in hospital because she experienced breathing difficulties. They looked after her so well. If I have a baby again, I would probably go there rather than wasting £15,000 at The Portland.

Because I'm in the public eye, people probably assume that I'm a bit of a snob when it comes to things like that. But like I said, if I'm lucky enough to do it again, I'll do it on the NHS.

The Royal Sussex County Hospital was fine, but it was a little bit run-down. The hospital is near the seafront and it was a miserable windy and rainy day. You wouldn't have thought it was May. It was absolutely freezing. The window was broken and people kept coming in and tying a sheet over it to stop it from banging. You definitely don't get that at The Portland! But I didn't care where I was. As long as my baby was delivered safely, that's all that mattered.

That morning, they put a pessary in me to try and trigger the birth because Harvey just wasn't budging. He was very snug inside my stomach. Maybe it would have been different if I was with someone at the time because apparently sex can trigger the birth. But I was single, so I had to settle for a pessary instead – which isn't quite the same! I also ate a curry the night before to try and get him out, but that didn't work. But then again, it was a chicken korma, which is probably the mildest curry you can get. Perhaps I should have gone for a vindaloo.

When I look back, I don't know why I didn't put my foot down because I'd never, ever let myself go almost two weeks overdue again. I sometimes question if that's why Harvey could be the way he is now because he was in me for too long. But there's no point worrying about the 'what-ifs', I suppose.

It got to about 2pm and absolutely nothing had happened. They decided to put another pessary in me, but again, still nothing. They were making me walk up and down the stairs to try and bring the labour on. I just kept thinking, 'Why is it not working?' I'm quite an impatient person, so I was getting extremely frustrated. They were pretty sure the first one would work, and it obviously didn't. So I was thinking, 'How much longer am I going to have to be in this bloody hospital?'

They finally told me they were going to break my waters. I thought it was going to happen quickly, but it didn't. They told me to get on the bed, lay on my back, open my legs and bend my knees. And then I just remember seeing what looked like a huge hook coming towards me and being put in me. I already felt uncomfortable that my legs were at quarter to three, never mind having a hook inside me. By the way, if you've never heard of the expression 'quarter to three', I just mean my legs were spread wide – like a clock at quarter to three.

My waters eventually broke and I thought to myself, 'Please don't tell me it gets any more painful than this.' Jesus, after knowing what came my way hours later, that was the understatement of the year! And then the contractions started.

Anyone who has given birth will know exactly what I mean by this – the only way I can describe the contractions is like waves in the sea. They start small, but then they build up and become bigger and bigger, to the point of extreme pain. And then you know they're going to go back down again and become calmer and feel better. And that goes on for hours. I was getting in and out of the birth pool and I kept telling them I wanted an epidural, but they were saying, 'No, you're doing so well. You don't need one yet. You're not far gone enough.'

I was in so much pain! My eyes felt like they were bulging out of my head. I just remember looking at the doctors and thinking, 'What is going on? This doesn't feel right.' I was holding on to the taps in the pool and screaming at the top of my lungs, 'When is this going to be over?' It was horrific. I'm not being dramatic, but I felt like I was going to die. I really felt like I couldn't take it any more. 'Why would any woman put herself through this again?!' I thought.

I was sitting on the toilet and I was one million per cent convinced that his head was hanging out of me. I kept asking them to check. It wasn't, but it was the strangest sensation.

I also just remember not wanting to get my hair wet in the pool because it goes really curly when it's wet. I had a hair cap on and my mum was patting my forehead with a wet sponge. I absolutely loved the feeling of the sponge against my skin, but I was being really particular about it. I kept shouting at her, 'Don't get my hair wet!' I can't believe I was even bothered about that! I knew I was going to look rough by the time Harvey made his appearance, but I thought that at least if my hair was half decent I wouldn't look so terrible in the first photos my mum was bound to take. How vain is that?!

I'd heard men say before that once they've seen their other halves giving birth, they don't ever look at *it* the same way again. Luckily, I didn't have a partner to say that, but I was really paranoid about the doctors looking at me. I just couldn't get the thought out of my head. I know it sounds silly, but I just thought they would be judging me because I was this pin-up girl and they'd go home and tell all their mates they'd seen Jordan's 'bits'. I know it's totally ridiculous and doctors don't even think about that, but I was convinced. I was adamant that I didn't want to give birth laying on my back with my legs open for everyone to see. Instead, I was squatting on all fours.

They gave me a pethidine injection to ease the pain. Even though I was in agony, I was absolutely terrified because I have a phobia of needles. And yes, despite all the surgery I've had, I still hate needles. They put it in my arse cheek and I just remember it burning. My arse was on fire! Or maybe that was just the curry I'd had the night before…

But I'm telling you now, it did absolutely sweet FA to help the pain. I was sucking on that gas and air like there was no tomorrow. I was making heaving noises because I couldn't get enough of it in me. But that wasn't doing anything for me, either. I swear they were just giving me air.

I kept saying to the midwives, 'Please don't talk.' I just wanted complete silence. Any small noise grated on me. The pain was getting more intense and all I wanted was an epidural. I asked again, but then they told me I'd gone too far to be able to have one. I just didn't know how much longer I was going to be able to deal with the pain.

When they told me he was nearly coming, I kept thinking, 'How on earth am I going to try and squeeze something the size of a melon out of me? Will I need stitches? Will it still look nice down there?' And then they told me they could see the head. They were trying to tell me what to do and when to push, but I wasn't really listening because when you're in that much pain, only you can be in control of your body.

Dwight was told all the details, so he knew I was going into the hospital to have the baby at 8am. He turned up later that day at around 6pm in the evening. He obviously thought that I would have had the baby by then, but I hadn't. I think he was hoping the later he left it, the more likely it was that everything would be over and done with.

He walked into the hospital with a bunch of flowers, a balloon and a big teddy bear. 'Why would he buy me fucking flowers?' I thought. It was definitely for the cameras because I knew for a fact it wasn't for me. It was obvious that he was trying to look good for the press because he had made it very clear he didn't want to know me or the baby. He was waiting outside with my mum and I asked him if he wanted to come in. Again, not because I wanted him with me, but because I didn't want our son to ever hold a grudge against me.

He could hear how much pain I was in, but he didn't want to come in so he stayed outside. My mum and Sally were absolutely brilliant with me throughout the birth, though. I'm surprised I didn't break their hands from squeezing them so hard. And oh my God, the noises I was making! It was like a werewolf was possessing my body. I really couldn't have done it without them.

I gave birth at 1.15am. It was such a traumatic birth. It's the worst pain I've ever experienced in my life. I will never forget it. I was absolutely exhausted and my eyes were all red and puffy. I was just completely knackered. They told me he would be a small baby, which is why they let me carry on with no pain relief. My arse! He wasn't small at all. They did say to me afterwards that if they knew he was going to be big then they would have done a caesarean because I had such a small frame. My hips could hardly carry him towards the end.

During my pregnancy, my grandad Harvey was really ill. That's where the name comes from – I wanted to name him after my grandad. He died not long after Harvey was born, but I was happy that he was able to meet him. My family loved Dwight, which I always found quite annoying after what he put me through. But my grandad was the only one who wasn't very keen on him. He always said to me that Dwight wouldn't stick around – and he was right.

I don't think he was very happy about the fact I was having a baby with Dwight as he was quite traditional. But in the end, he actually became really excited about the pregnancy and couldn't wait for me to have the baby. He adored Harvey and he was so proud that he was named after him. I also gave him the middle name Daniel after my older brother.

My perfect Harvey Daniel Price was born on Monday 27 May 2002, weighing 8lbs 7oz, and that's where our journey begins…

Two

WELCOME TO THE WORLD

I couldn't stop looking at Harvey as he laid on my chest. I was totally in love and I felt an instant bond. 'How have I created this perfect little human?' I thought as I stroked his soft, chubby cheek.

He was such a gorgeous looking baby. He had big, brown, beautiful eyes and plump lips – they were so red and cute. My mum and Sally were crying, which then set me off. But they were happy tears, of course. I just couldn't believe he was finally here and he was mine.

He looked exactly like what I imagined a baby should look like. Sometimes newborns can look wrinkly and have scrunched-up faces like little old men, but he didn't.

Throughout my pregnancy, I often imagined the moment I'd first meet my baby and what he would look like. I don't know why, but I pictured him coming out with loads of Afro hair. But he didn't have much hair at all. He also had a perfectly round head. A lot of babies sometimes come out looking like a character out of the 90s film *Coneheads*, not that I've ever seen it myself. He was just so beautiful and I felt like the luckiest person in the world.

The midwives were busy cleaning up around us and after the chaos of the birth, I felt totally at peace with Harvey. Now that he was actually in my arms, I finally understood why women choose to put themselves through childbirth again. All the pain is worth it. Although I definitely don't agree with people who say you forget the pain because 19 years later, I certainly haven't.

Harvey didn't cry much – he seemed so laid-back. It felt amazing holding him and breathing in that lovely newborn smell. If I could take that scent, bottle it up and make it into a perfume, I would. I felt on top of the world. It was an incredible feeling – and such a relief. Finally, I had my perfect baby boy.

More of my family had arrived at the hospital and Dwight eventually came into the room to meet his son. It was time to cut the umbilical cord and I asked if he wanted to do it. No matter how I felt about Dwight, he was the dad after all. He didn't want to because he said he didn't like blood, so my dad cut the cord instead.

When I look back, I just think, if he didn't want anything to do with him, why did he even bother turning up at the hospital? To be honest, I think it's because he was this big famous footballer and he was advised to come by his manager otherwise he'd get bad press.

We changed Harvey into some clothes and Dwight asked why he had bruises on his body. I had no idea what he was going on about. It was like he was trying to insinuate that I'd dropped him or something. He made me feel like complete shit. I later realised that he was actually referring to Harvey's Mongolian blue spots, which are common in babies with darker skin.

Harvey was also wearing a little knitted hat to match his outfit and Dwight turned around and said to me, 'It's too hot in here. Take the hat off.' He then saw a bottle at the side of the bed and started telling me I should be breastfeeding Harvey. I felt like saying, 'Why don't you fuck off?' When he started talking like that, I told him to leave and take his shit flowers and bear with him. But really, they weren't shit at all. They were actually really nice flowers, but I wasn't going to tell him that!

It was such a weird atmosphere. In a conventional world, Mum and Dad are in the room bonding with the baby and you feel more in love than ever. But having the dad in the room had the opposite effect on me – Dwight made me cry. I'd gone from happy tears to sad tears in the space of a few minutes. It was like he was only there to have a go at me. He made me feel like utter shit.

I didn't even get a 'well done' from him for what I'd just done. I'd welcomed his son into the world for God's sake! To put it bluntly, he was a rude, arrogant prick. There were a lot of things I wanted to say, but I thought to myself, 'Don't start an argument now, Katie. Just get him out.' I was absolutely exhausted and I just wanted to be left alone so I could rest with Harvey.

When the time came, I was glad to be leaving the hospital and going home. But before I did, something else had pissed me off. I know I was hormonal, but I had every reason to be annoyed. I had breakfast TV on in the background. They were going through the morning papers and having a discussion about the top headlines. I wasn't really paying much attention, but my ears pricked up when the conversation turned to my new baby – and they started slagging me off.

I was used to people slating me, but now that I actually had Harvey in my arms, it cut deep and I felt defensive. I hadn't even brought him home yet and people were already judging me as a mum. If anything, it just pushed me to prove everyone wrong.

As we left the hospital, the press were outside trying

to get pictures of Harvey. My dad brought the car straight to the door so I could jump in and leave as quickly as possible to avoid the swarm of paparazzi. My manager Dave helped me cover up the car seat to stop them getting any pictures of his face. It was crazy! I expected a bit of press attention, but this was insane. I definitely wasn't as clued-up back then as I am now.

I was really careful and made sure not to show Harvey's face. I was due to do a shoot with *OK! Magazine* and had signed an exclusive deal with them which meant I was giving them the first pictures. I ended up doing the shoot just ten days after having Harvey, and I really don't know how I got through it. I was still in a lot of pain from the birth, but I was excited. I couldn't wait to show him off to the world.

My film crew were also documenting my every move. People still ask me now what it's like filming my life, but it's something I've always done and loved. If the public didn't support me and I didn't get viewing figures, I wouldn't be here 20-odd years later. So it's all down to them – and I'm very grateful for that.

I must be doing something right. I won *Celebrity Big Brother* in 2015 and to win a show like that, you have to get the public's vote. So the public obviously must like me. Sometimes I do question what it is that makes me different from everyone else. Most people who were big in the press at the same time as I was aren't still making headlines today. Maybe it's because my life really is like a soap opera. But one thing I know for certain is that people can relate to me because I go through real-life dramas.

I'm just myself and I'm not manufactured. I hope that I've been an inspiration for other people to never give up. If there are any young girls reading this and they find themselves in a similar situation to what I was in – pregnant and facing life as a single mum – then honestly, just do what you want to do and do what feels right.

Don't be pressured into doing things you don't want to do and don't be influenced by other people. A lot of women end up having terminations because they think they don't have the money, the house or the ideal family set-up. But trust me, you always find a way. Everyone's circumstances are different and I can only speak from my own experience, but I wouldn't change anything about my life with Harvey. If I could go back in time, I'd tell that vulnerable, confused and scared girl at the abortion clinic not to worry. Having a baby is a guaranteed unconditional love and bond. It's just an unbelievable, indescribable feeling.

My house still wasn't quite finished when I had Harvey, so I lived with my mum until he was about three months old and we moved in when it was ready for us. The first weeks with Harvey were lovely and I was really embracing motherhood. I think even my mum was surprised at how well I was coping.

But don't get me wrong, I also found it quite overwhelming. I had a lot of visits from family and friends in the beginning, which I loved, but at the same time, I hated. Everyone wanted to hold Harvey, but I just didn't want anyone touching him. It sounds awful, but I used to make up excuses so that they couldn't. If he was awake, I'd say I was just trying to get him to sleep so I wanted to leave him be. Or if he was asleep, I'd say he's just gone to bed and ask them not to disturb him. When really, I was just being a selfish cow who wanted him all to herself.

The only people I'd let hold him were my mum, dad, sister, brother and Sally. I remained very possessive over him and didn't let people hold him for months. I think it's because I've always longed for love – and I'd finally found it with Harvey. I didn't want anything to happen to him.

During this time, I also had a stalker, which was absolutely terrifying. I had to kit out my new house so that I had a trusty security system. I ended up having to get a huge fence, CCTV cameras, alarms and even panic buttons connected to the police station. I know it all sounds very dramatic, but I didn't feel safe. And I wasn't just protecting myself, I had to protect my son, too.

This random guy was sending me letter after

letter, claiming that he knew me and that we were in a relationship. It was gut-wrenching stuff. I'd had my fair share of hate mail, but this was scary. I felt like I was constantly looking over my shoulder whenever I went out. I tried to brush the letters off, but then he turned up at my mum's house, which really freaked us all out. I ended up having to get a restraining order to stop him from coming anywhere near me.

Along with nutters, I also found the paparazzi very hard to deal with. I was used to them following me around because of my career, but after I had Harvey, it started a whole new level that I'd never experienced before – and it's continued ever since.

That's why I've been banned from driving multiple times now. I'm currently waiting to get my licence back. If I'm speeding, it's because I'm trying to get away from the paps. They were constantly outside the house trying to take pictures of me with Harvey. Even while I was pregnant, my friends would have to tell them to go away because they were stressing me out and I was worried about what it could do to the baby. But they didn't care. I understand they have a job to do and have food to put on the table like we all do, and I had a good relationship with the paps. But this was crossing a line.

The press didn't stop there. Before I'd even got Harvey's birth certificate, there were headlines in the papers saying, 'He's too white to be Dwight's.' Come on, you can't deny the fact Harvey is Dwight's. He looks exactly like him.

Looking back, I can't believe they were allowed to even say that. It's so racist – and it was front-page news! What the press put me through was so cruel and it really did affect me. There would just be constant untrue stories and there was nothing I could do about it. I used to think, 'How can you even begin to argue against a national paper?' I didn't have a chance!

If it was this day and age, you can fight back on social media and set the record straight. Now, when false stories come out, I can go on my social media platforms and name and shame a journalist or a publication. They then beg me to take it down because my right of reply reaches more people than the amount of people who buy their papers or magazines. That must cut really deep! But my point is, if you're going to do a story on me, make sure you've got your facts right and you're not just relying on a 'source'.

I don't know why they don't just ask me straight out because I've always been honest. But I am flattered that stories about me still sell. Back in those days, I had no right of reply. My publicist might have denied stories, but the press didn't care. They would run it anyway. I just had to let people read the headlines, and most people probably did believe them. Harvey did have light skin, but so what? It didn't mean he wasn't Dwight's.

I felt hurt because they were basically calling me a slag and people were questioning who the dad was. That's how I started to get the reputation that I slept around. But I can tell you now, I know exactly how many people I've slept with. And at that point, I could count the amount of guys I'd slept with on one hand.

Just because I had a job as a glamour model, it doesn't mean I was a slag. I was a totally different person to the way I was being portrayed in the media. In actual fact, I was a late bloomer. I didn't go clubbing until I was older, I didn't have a boyfriend until I was older and I didn't lose my virginity until I was older. When I look back, I suppose I can see why people would have judged me. But I was young and I was just living my life and going out like everyone else.

According to the papers, all I had to do was speak to a guy and that automatically meant that I'd slept with them. I found it hard to meet people because they thought I was intimidating from what they'd read about me. They presumed I'd be a certain type of person, but really, I was very family oriented and I was just focused on my horses. Yeah, I had a good body, I had money and I was a pretty good catch if I do say so myself, but I like to think I'm very down to earth.

At the end of the day, I was bringing up a child as a single parent. I wasn't harming anyone, so I didn't understand why the press couldn't just leave me alone. Rant over!

Dwight didn't really have any involvement with us until Harvey had to be registered. I kept reminding him we needed to do it before he turned six weeks old, but he kept putting it off. He finally agreed to come with me and I felt so relieved because I really wanted him there.

He'd already missed out on so much, but I would have been furious if he'd missed this. But this is Dwight we're talking about, so it didn't go as smooth sailing as I'd hoped.

As I was on my way to the register office, he told me he'd spoken to his lawyers – and then he asked me to do a DNA test. He said he was advised not to put his name on the certificate unless there was proof Harvey was his.

'Why the hell do you want a DNA test? He's yours!' I said. This was so typical of Dwight. He demanded a test, so I told him not to bother coming. I said to him, 'If you want to be on the birth certificate, turn up at the register office, and if you don't, then don't.'

I stood my ground and I refused to give him a DNA test. In the end, he did put his name on the certificate. This is what I still can't understand about Dwight. He wasn't involved in the pregnancy, yet he turned up to the birth. He was advised not to be on the birth certificate, but he still turned up and did it. I think it's because deep down, he knew Harvey was his.

Even though he came along, we weren't talking at all. It was so awkward. We didn't say a word to each other. You could cut the tension with a knife. The woman in the register office must have thought, 'What on earth is going on?'

And then we got into another argument because he wanted to name him Eversley, which is Dwight's middle name. 'No way,' I said. 'I'm calling him Harvey Daniel.' He hadn't been there throughout the pregnancy or the birth, so he didn't have a choice. He also wanted his surname to be Yorke, but there was no fucking way I was letting that happen. As if I was going to give Harvey his name after the way he'd treated us. I think he knew he didn't have a leg to stand on, because when the woman asked us to clarify Harvey's name, Dwight just shrugged and said nothing.

In the whole 19 years of Harvey's life, Dwight must have seen him about ten times. To this day, I'm not sure whether during one of those times he secretly took something from Harvey and did his own DNA test. If I'm being completely honest, I reckon he probably did, but I have no idea and I never will.

Dwight doesn't pay anything towards Harvey either.

In the beginning, he had to by law. It was around £1,300 a month. When we were trying to make the arrangements, I just remember his lawyers asking me all sorts of questions about really specific things. They were asking what kind of bed sheets I'd bought for Harvey and the type of nappies he had so that they could add it all up and come up with an accurate price. It was so petty. I couldn't really be arsed with it, but I thought, 'Actually, no. He's Dwight's son as well as mine and it's also his responsibility to pay for him.'

But it didn't last long. He kept missing payments and after about a year and a half, if that, they stopped completely. To this day, I haven't asked him for another penny. Even though I'm completely within my rights to do so. Although I wish I had now because I could have done with some Chanel and Louis Vuitton bags! That's a joke, by the way. But after the way he's acted, I think he owes me more than just a couple of designer bags.

Harvey has been a very expensive baby because of his disabilities. I could go back to him now and demand money if I wanted to, which sometimes I do feel like doing. It's not for me, it's for Harvey. I just feel like Dwight has completely got away with it scot-free.

But I also heard that he almost faced bankruptcy. It's really sad if that's the case because he had so much money. He's a typical footballer – they spend their money because they think it'll last forever. I don't agree with what Dwight has done and is still doing to Harvey, but it is horrible to see that for anyone.

No matter how much of an idiot Dwight was acting, I had Harvey and that's all that mattered. Our bond was unbelievable. I'd have him in bed with me all the time and I never let him go.

I was in a lot of pain for the first few weeks. Going to the toilet was excruciating. The way I describe the feeling to people is like putting salt and vinegar on a graze, but down below. These are the things people don't tell you about having a baby. Harvey has been my only natural baby because I told myself I'd never do it again after that horrific birth. I had caesareans with all the others. I used to watch *One Born Every Minute* and think, 'How on earth did I ever do that?!'

The health visitor came over to see us for the first time – and I could tell that she knew who I was. She didn't say anything, but she didn't have to. I could tell by her mannerisms that she was judging me. I was obviously in the press and known as a party girl.

I'd hardly said a word and she turned around and said to me, 'You mustn't swear in front of him.' I was thinking, 'What do you mean, swear in front of him? He's just been born!' She made me feel like shit. The woman had literally just walked into the house and I'd given her no reason to judge me like that. Obviously it got my back up because people have judged me from a young age. I was a Page Three girl who had just had a baby with a footballer and I was doing it on my own, so I guess there was a stigma attached to it.

Because I have a younger sister, I knew what it was like to have a baby in the family, so I did have some experience. If I'm being honest, I think half of the time, a lot of health visitors don't even have kids themselves and they have no idea what it's like. They can make first-time mums feel like nervous wrecks.

There's no textbook on how to be a mum. Yes, there should be someone in place after you've had a baby to check the weight and whether they're feeding right, but when it comes to how you bring your child up, it's actually none of their business as long as they're loved.

A newborn just wants to be watered, fed, changed, cuddled and put down to sleep. They're the basic things anyone needs to know. But like any mum, I went and bought everything. You name it – I had it. When I look back now, I didn't need half the shit I bought. But when it's your first, you think you need everything.

I can tell you now, after having five children, the advice the health visitors give you changes constantly anyway. They gave me conflicting advice with all my kids, so I just did it my way in the end. To get them to sleep, I used to wrap them all up like little cocoons so that they felt like they were constantly being cuddled. They tell you to use cotton wool and water rather than baby wipes for the first few months. They also tell you not to bathe them every day. I did the complete opposite with my last three – and they're all completely fine. Maybe I should bring out my own baby book next!

On the subject of babies, there are a lot of things I wish I knew beforehand. So for anyone who wants to know – the umbilical cord is disgusting. Your belly button sticks out and then it goes all gooey like snot before it falls off. It's so gross. And oh my God, it smells vile! Another thing I had no idea about was baby poo. No one ever told me their first poo is black like tar! I got the shock of my life when I changed Harvey's nappy for the first time. I thought something was seriously wrong.

The health visitor came to see us a few times. Harvey's weight was fine. He actually lost weight at first, which is normal for newborn babies. As far as I was concerned, he was completely healthy. He was feeding well and everything seemed to be fine.

Then it came to his six-week check-up – and that's when my world turned upside down.

Three

THE DAY EVERYTHING CHANGED

I was in such a baby bubble and I'd never been happier in my whole life. It's crazy how your life can go from one extreme to the other in a split second.

The health visitor checked Harvey's eyes as part of the standard routine, and I'll never forget the expression on her face when she put the torch in his eyes. 'He doesn't seem to be following the light,' she said. 'Have you noticed him following your face? And does he smile back at you?'

He used to smile at me, but to be honest, I wasn't sure if it was just because he had wind. When they're newborns, you just assume they're looking at you. I guess I didn't really think about it. She was asking me whether he had been following his baby mobile, but I didn't really know the answer. You've been told your baby is healthy, so you don't expect to be told anything is wrong.

She said she was concerned about his eyes and that he may not be able to see, but told me not to be worried about it because some babies can just be late at developing things. She told us to go to our local doctor for a second opinion. When she left, I explained to my mum what she'd just said. We were both frantically looking at his eyes. As far as we could tell, it seemed like he was looking at us and following us. My mum had loads of experience with children and she didn't think anything was wrong. But of course, my mum being my mum, she was on my case to make a doctor's appointment straight away, which I did. And my mum was with me every step of the way.

In the days leading up to the appointment, I was just looking into Harvey's eyes constantly. But to be honest, I didn't even know what I was meant to be looking at. He was only six weeks old, and I was convinced he couldn't have anything wrong with him.

The wait for the appointment felt like forever. I was having sleepless nights, worrying about what could be wrong with my perfect little Harvey. I saw my local GP, Dr Khan, who has been our family doctor for years. My mum and dad still know him now. I've heard he's gone grey. (If you're reading this Dr Khan, you know my cheeky side very well and you know that I'm only teasing you. Also, thank you for all the years you've looked after me and my family – and for being gentle in the way you noticed there was a problem with Harvey's eyes.)

He checked Harvey and, like the health visitor, he also said he didn't seem to be following properly with his eyes. He told us that actually, it wasn't common and it was unusual for his age.

I instantly thought the worst. My mum said, 'Be positive. You don't know anything yet.' But I'm the complete opposite to my mum in that sense. I admire her optimism, but in any situation I always prepare for the worst. So Dr Khan referred us to the Ear, Nose And Throat department. When your local doctor, who you've known for most of your life, is telling you that something is unusual, you know there's something to be worried about. Especially when you're referred so quickly. I think we got seen within about a week.

My mum came along with us again for the appointment. We were sitting in the waiting room and I was feeling so anxious because I knew I was finally going to find out what was wrong with Harvey's eyes.

It's a surreal situation to be in because you know as soon as you walk through the door, you're going to be walking out with an answer – whether it's good or bad. In all honesty, at the time, I had an overwhelming feeling that it was going to be bad, and I'm very rarely wrong. But now, through my knowledge about eyes and Harvey's complex needs, I really had nothing to worry about. When your child has a disability, it's just a different kind of love and care that you give to them. Nothing is perfect and normal in this world. But actually, Harvey is perfect in every way to me.

The doctor got out his torch and looked into Harvey's eyes. There were a few 'ums' and 'ahs', and that was it. That was when they dropped the bombshell.

'He's blind,' he said.

It was very matter of fact. 'What do you mean he's blind? How can he be blind?!' I thought. 'Fuck. What kind of life is he going to have?' I felt broken.

We had all these questions to ask, but it felt like we were on a conveyor belt and it was time for the next patient to be seen. We didn't really have any time to process it. We were just sitting there waiting for the doctor to give us leaflets or some information about places we could visit for support, but there was nothing. I suppose when I look back, what could he have done? There were no places we could have gone to for help, but we just felt completely shit and helpless.

Neither of us cried at that moment. We were just in

total shock. I'd look at my perfect baby and think, 'How on earth is he blind?' I couldn't believe it. 'He's never going to be independent,' I thought. 'He's never going to be able to live a proper life.' I never could have imagined that something like this would happen.

To this day, I've never actually sat and cried about it. Don't get me wrong, there have been many times I could have easily broken down into tears, but we're quite good as a family at dealing with things. Because I was young and had dealt with loads of shit in the press already, I guess I had a wall up. 'Just get on with it,' I'd tell myself. But I still had so many unanswered questions. How did anyone not know Harvey was blind in the beginning? And what has caused it?

When it came out in the press that Harvey was blind, there were so many stories blaming me for my partying. As I said, I'd already been accused of drinking while I was pregnant, so this just made it ten times worse. I really felt like the press were having a field day.

I was even accused of taking drugs in my pregnancy, which is just ridiculous. When you're pregnant, you have blood tests and you're tested for everything, so it obviously wasn't true.

A couple of years ago I was self-medicating on cocaine before I checked myself into The Priory for post-traumatic stress disorder. I think the main trigger was getting held at gunpoint in South Africa in 2018 in front of Junior and Princess. I don't know how we survived it. At the same time, the media was picking on me. All the false stories had finally gotten on top of me and it became too much. I needed help and it's the best decision I've ever made. And now I know that if I ever get to that place again, I can get help. I always say that if I have that feeling tapping me on my shoulder, I'd be able to recognise it and go to the doctor.

But isn't that sad how nothing has changed in 20 years? The press were making things up about me then, and they still do it now. A lot of people ask me why I don't just sue them if what they're writing is inaccurate. But it's not as simple as that. The only people who win in that situation are the lawyers because you spend loads of money trying to rectify the stories, and most of the time, all you get is a tiny apology that people don't even see anyway.

I was even set up with drugs once. Before I was pregnant, I was at the Laureus World Sports Awards in Monte Carlo with Dwight. I was befriended by a journalist – I didn't know her job title at the time. She was being overly friendly and hanging around with me all night, which I later discovered was because she was doing a massive story on me.

I remember going into the toilet with her and she offered me cocaine. 'No, I don't do it,' I said. Imagine if

I'd have done it? Thank God I didn't. It could have been career ruining for me. Also, I found out she later went on a private boat with Dwight while I was left to go back to the hotel on my own, and he'd asked her for a threesome with one of his mates. How disgusting.

After that, I made an excuse to fly home. When I look back, I was actually pregnant with Harvey that night without knowing. I will admit now that I looked absolutely hideous. I had horrible hair extensions, huge lips and a tacky pink outfit. I looked proper trashy!

But yeah, all these stories were coming out about me and the media were ruthless. I was even called 'the mother from hell' in some newspapers, which was the most hurtful thing anyone could ever say to me. But little did they know that years later I'd be voted Celebrity Mum Of The Year. So ha! It was a really nice feeling to know that people realised how important my kids are to me. At the same time, it's not like I need an award to prove I'm a good mum. But it was still good to win it.

The stories were really making me suffer, but I put on a brave face. It was just me and Harvey, and I had to be strong for him. I felt like shit and I still had no proper answers about Harvey and what had caused his blindness. At home, me and my mum would just constantly look at him. I became obsessed with looking at his eyes. They would move slowly and I was always showing him things and trying to interact with him. I'd think, 'I know I can get his eyesight back. Surely he can't be permanently blind.' I kept closing my eyes and trying to imagine what it was like for Harvey to just see complete darkness. I felt so sad for him and his future.

Not long after, I also got my own devastating diagnosis. I was told I had cancer. But it felt like a drop in the ocean compared to what Harvey was going through. At this point, I didn't really care what happened to me, I just wanted my son to be okay.

While I was pregnant, I noticed a lump on my index finger while I was getting a manicure. I was convinced it was from a horse riding accident I'd had a few days before. And yes, you can still ride a horse when you're pregnant. My horse basically reversed into a pole and bolted off with me while I was on it. Through all my years of horse-riding experience, that had never happened before. I was quite far gone in my pregnancy, so it was terrifying.

All I could think was, 'How the hell am I going to stop the horse?' Anyway, I did stop the horse and I luckily managed to escape with minimal injuries. So I just presumed the lump was from knocking my hand during that.

I went to the doctor's surgery, but I couldn't get it X-rayed because I was pregnant. Unfortunately Dr Khan wasn't available at the time, so I saw another doctor who told me it wasn't serious. I kept an eye on it over the next few months and the lump became bigger and bigger. It didn't hurt, but it was in an awkward position. It was just annoying, more than anything.

My mum was pushing for me to get it checked again, so once I had Harvey, I finally went for the X-ray and I was referred to a specialist. Within a couple of weeks I had the lump removed and it was sent to America to be examined. The results came back, and that's when I was told the news. The doctor sat me down, and I could tell straight away by his face that something wasn't right. Then he came out with it.

'I've got bad news, it's leiomyosarcoma – a form of cancer,' he said. When you hear that word, you just feel completely numb. I phoned my mum to tell her and I just said in a flippant kind of way, 'Don't worry about it. I'll call you back later.' I didn't want her to panic. We were already going through so much stress, I didn't want to make her poorly. I just thought, 'Here we go. Another thing to deal with. What's going to be thrown at me next?'

The doctor reoperated on my finger because they wanted to get right to the root of it and make sure there was no cancerous tissue left. He actually warned me that I might lose my finger during the operation. So I was very happy to have five fingers still intact afterwards.

I had to have regular check-ups for the next six years

and thankfully, everything came back clear. The doctor told me that it was the pregnancy that had actually triggered the signs, otherwise it could have stayed dormant in my body.

The kind of cancer that I had develops in fatty tissue and can spread to your insides. I count my lucky stars that it showed as a lump, otherwise it could have been too late. It's a rare type of cancer. Around 600 people in the UK are diagnosed with it every year and in its advanced stages, it has a 50 per cent survival rate. When I asked if the cancer could have been the cause of Harvey's blindness, the doctor reassured me it definitely wasn't.

At the time, I remember thinking, 'Bloody hell, there's so much drama going on in my life.' And as the years have gone by, the drama just hasn't stopped.

People have made money from my misfortune by selling stories on me. After leaving The Priory, I've cut negative people out of my life and kept my circle very small. It's taken me years to work out the press… and I still haven't properly worked it out. But I certainly know that I've learnt to be more in control. I've tried keeping things private, but because I'm so open and honest, I find it hard.

While all this drama was going on, I was still filming my reality show. At the time, Hugh Hefner wanted me to do *Playboy*. And yes, it was the proper *Playboy* – the

American one. It makes me laugh so much when girls say they've done *Playboy*, but what they really mean is they've done it for other countries.

If you're going to do *Playboy*, it's got to be the American one to be credible. And you've actually got to make it onto the cover of the magazine and meet Hugh – that's the ultimate goal.

I was going through shit, but I didn't want to miss out on such an amazing experience. It was an opportunity of a lifetime. Besides, there was no point moping around at home feeling sorry for myself.

So me, Mum and Harv flew to America so that I could visit the mansion and do my *Playboy* shoot. In fact, I didn't just visit the mansion, I actually lived in it. It was insane!

I'd imagined the mansion would be like some kind of exotic boudoir – *Fifty Shades Of Grey* style. But it was nothing like that. My bedroom was tastefully decorated and I had a stunning view of the grounds. I'd wake up in the morning, dial reception on the phone for room service, order myself some porridge for breakfast, open the curtains and look out onto the huge swimming pool – which would always be full of glamorous bunnies sunbathing. Ah, what a life!

I absolutely loved my shoot. I revealed more than I ever had before, but the pictures weren't pornographic or anything like that. It was a nice distraction from reality, even if it was only for a little while.

We were in America for about six weeks and while we were over there, we booked Harvey in to see one of the top eye specialists in Los Angeles to get another opinion. It's so typical of me, trying to fit everything in at one time.

My mum was staying at The Standard hotel with Harv, while I was in the mansion with Hugh. Even writing that down feels surreal. I was taking my son to America with my mum to see an eye doctor, but I was also staying in the *Playboy* mansion with Hugh. You couldn't write it! Any sane person would go somewhere local or pay to go privately, but nope, not me. I decided to get on a plane and travel all the way to America.

I'd obviously still see my mum and Harvey while I was there, but me and the other girls would go out every Monday, Wednesday and Friday night. One of the nights, we were in the car with Hugh on our way to a club, which was underneath The Standard where my mum was staying.

I said to Hugh, 'Let's go knock on the door and you can meet my mum and my son.' So us girls walked across the hotel lobby in our little bunny outfits with Hugh and turned up at my mum's door. She was in bed and she must have thought, 'What on earth is going on?' But she let us in and that's when Hugh met Harvey. What an experience that was! I've still got pictures somewhere of Hugh and Harvey together.

The day arrived for us to see the eye specialist. I remember thinking it would be this huge, fancy hospital, but it was just a small place in a tall building. America is completely different to England. There are rows of office blocks with lots of different rooms for different things. So in one room was the eye specialist, and then across the corridor could be a completely separate company. Even having surgery in America is very different to England, but that's another story!

The doctor tested Harvey's eyes, and again, it was all very matter of fact. 'Yes. He's blind. I'm afraid he's not going to be able to see,' she told us. As she was known for being such a good eye specialist, I thought I was going to get more of a reason as to how this had happened. I'll never forget what she said next. 'You shouldn't mix Black and White,' she told us.

'What do you mean?' I said. I was completely stunned. And she just simply said, 'This is what happens when you're a White woman with a Black man.'

Me and my mum couldn't believe what we were hearing. How disgusting is that? She made me feel so small. Normally, I'd react and say something back because I find it hard to bite my tongue. But after just having it confirmed to me that Harvey was definitely blind, her cruel comment was actually the last thing on my mind. The first thing on my mind was phoning Dwight to tell him the news because I wanted to keep him in the loop.

I don't know why, but I suppose I also wanted some kind of reassurance from him, as he is the dad after all. All I wanted to hear was, 'It will all be okay. He's still our beautiful boy.' But no. Straight away he turned on me. 'It's all your fault my son is like this,' he said. 'He's never going to be able to play golf or football.'

He blamed me for everything and I felt shit. I couldn't be bothered to argue. I thought, 'Fuck you. He's my son, so you can fuck off.' I knew it wasn't my fault because I was actually tested at Great Ormond Street, just to put my mind at ease. They did lots of blood tests on me and reassured me that Harvey's condition is a one-in-a-million chance. But that still doesn't stop you from worrying.

It was playing on my mind because I admit that I had used sunbeds while I was pregnant. I was always told it was safe to do so while pregnant, but I wondered whether the UV light could have affected him. But it hadn't. The hospital told me that even if I'd been drinking alcohol throughout my pregnancy, it wouldn't have made a difference to his condition.

As well as putting my own mind at rest, I suppose I also wanted to have the proof in writing – just in case I ever needed it after what the papers were saying about me. The doctors were actually really interested in the genetic side of it because they had no explanation as to why it happens. I've had more blood tests through the years so they can use it as research. I hope one day they're able to find an answer.

So that was that. I'd seen a handful of doctors, all with the same opinion, and Harvey was definitely blind. My mum kept saying, 'He'll be able to see at some point,' but I had to bluntly tell her, 'No Mum. He's blind.' I felt bad for snapping at her, but there was no point in kidding ourselves.

It was never picked up throughout the pregnancy. I'm not sure with today's technology whether doctors are actually able to see the optic nerve in the eye on the scan, but they definitely couldn't back then. We were in complete shock about it all, but we had to get on with it. Even though my mum's optimism was slightly grating on me, she was so good with everything and she really did keep me going throughout that time.

When we got back to England, she was researching charities and she found Blatchington Court Trust, who we're still in touch with now. It's based in Sussex and it's for children who are blind and have special needs. It's where we met other mums, like Jeannette and her son Zack. Although we don't see them often, Zack is the boy who appeared on Harvey's BBC documentary, *Harvey And Me*.

Harvey got to about six months old. He was drinking so much and he was such a chubby baby. At this point, all I knew was that he was blind. But during the night he was constantly wanting to drink, which seemed weird. He was my firstborn so I didn't really have much to compare him to, but I knew it didn't seem right.

He had his own room, but it got to the point where I'd be up all the time giving him his bottle. So in the end, I'd have him in the bed with me and I'd fill bottles up and plant them on the headboard just so that I could lay in bed feeding him all night long without getting up and down. I was absolutely exhausted, but you just get used to it because you have to. You don't have any other choice. I was a single mum, so it's not like I could take it in turns with my partner.

I had a really busy work schedule and I was running on empty. It's not like I was having sleepless nights because he was crying all night long, it was just that he constantly needed feeding. In fact, I can't remember ever having to get up with Harvey to rock him back to sleep like I did with all my other babies. He was very quiet and the only time he ever cried was for his bottle. He was a very easy and placid baby. He was an absolute dream.

I noticed that he was getting ill quite often. Again, I had nothing to compare him to, but it seemed unusual. He'd have a high temperature as if he had a cold, so I was always giving him Calpol. But it never made him any better.

I took him to the doctor's surgery because I was concerned, but they couldn't find anything wrong. Whenever we visited Blatchington Court, the mums could see he was drinking a lot. I'd mentioned to them how I was constantly up in the night to give him his bottle, and how he kept getting poorly.

One of them suggested that I should get Harvey referred to a doctor because she thought that he could have something called diabetes insipidus, which is what her child had. It's a condition which causes an imbalance of fluids in the body and makes you incredibly thirsty. 'I don't think so,' I said. 'My local doctor said he was fine.' But she insisted and told me that I should try and get him referred to a doctor called Dr Dattani at Great Ormond Street. So I went back to Dr Khan and he referred us. You can't just turn up at Great Ormond Street. Anyone who goes there has to be referred by a doctor, which I never knew.

Dr Dattani was literally a lifesaver for us. As soon as we saw him, he knew exactly what was wrong with Harvey. He told me that Harvey did have diabetes insipidus, just like the mum had said.

He also diagnosed him with septo-optic dysplasia, which affects the optic nerve and causes blindness and growth-hormone deficiency because the pituitary gland doesn't function properly.

It was a lot to take in, but I finally had an answer. I'd been told Harvey was blind, but now that I'd been given a name for the condition, I felt like I could process it and understand it a bit more.

Dr Dattani is still involved in Harvey's life now. Sometimes I think to myself, 'If Harvey hadn't been referred, what would have happened?' I can't even bear to think about it, but he probably would have deteriorated rapidly and become very, very ill. I'm just so grateful we met the mums and Dr Dattani when we did. It just goes to show that there is always support and advice out there, no matter how helpless you feel. Never suffer in silence, and keep fighting until you get answers.

Dr Dattani did lots of tests on Harvey, and we realised that the hospital had made errors. Basically, they did an MRI scan on Harvey and told us that his optic nerve was too short. The optic nerve sends a message from the eye to the brain, which is why he can't see. But when we looked back, they only looked at his eyes. If they'd have looked at the pituitary gland, they would have known that it was abnormal.

If they'd have picked up on it earlier, he might not be quite how he is today. He was basically starved from medication that would have helped him at a younger age. We complained to the hospital and they admitted negligence. I could have sued them, but I knew that Harvey would need hospital care for the rest of his life so I didn't want to take it any further. And at the end of the day, it's not going to make Harvey any better. It wouldn't change anything and I didn't think it was worth the stress.

Dr Dattani put Harvey on a medication called DDAVP, also known as desmopressin acetate, which he's still on to this day. It basically controls the waterworks in your body and helps with the feeling of being constantly thirsty. When he was first prescribed it, I remember thinking, 'There's not much of a tablet there. Surely it won't make much of a difference.' It literally looked like a quarter of a tablet, but my God, it made a huge difference. I'll go into the details of Harvey's medication later on in the book, but it's crazy how such a small dose can have such a big effect. It's quite scary, actually. I find it really interesting.

Dr Dattani also referred us to Moorfields Eye Hospital, so we could regularly see the doctors there. At this point, we were still unaware of Harvey's other conditions. I thought that was that, and I was so relieved that we were finally on the right path with Dr Dattani.

Little did I know, it would only be the beginning.

Four

WORKING MUM

Harvey might have been more complex than other babies, but I was really taking motherhood in my stride. Although I was still growing up myself, I had to grow up much quicker for Harvey's sake. But he's never stopped me from doing the things I wanted to do, especially in my career. I'd always say to anyone that there's never a right or wrong time to have a baby, because they just fit into your life. No matter what, you just make it work.

For the first couple of years, Harvey came absolutely everywhere with me. It was always just me and him, and I loved every single minute of it. I never struggled. I took him to work with me all the time and my career kept me sane. I made sure that I was constantly busy so that I didn't have time to sit at home worrying about anything.

I had modelling shoots booked in and I was doing personal appearances in nightclubs. I wanted to earn as much money as I could so that I could give Harvey everything he needed. I felt like a proper grown-up. I had my own house, my own child, and I was now working to provide for him, not just me. I've never had an extravagant lifestyle, though. Not back then and certainly not now. I don't live above my means. Well, at least I don't think I do. Others may say otherwise!

My first glamour shoot after having Harvey was with *Loaded Magazine*. To this day, it's one of the best shoots I've ever done. I wanted to prove to people that I hadn't lost my figure and I was still at the top of my game.

For the shoot, I wore a white crop top and a little pink G-string. It felt so good to be back, and it was the best my body had ever looked – and it was only about six weeks after giving birth. I even went topless to show that my boobs were still perky. I can't believe how quickly my body snapped back into shape without me even trying. If anything, I was even smaller than I was before. I was still eating whatever I wanted, it's not like I was following a strict diet of chicken and vegetables. But I guess I'd lost some weight due to the stress and worry of what I was going through with Harvey. I didn't put much weight on throughout the pregnancy – I was all belly. My stomach was massive by the end, but if you saw me from behind, you wouldn't have even known I was pregnant.

Harvey was such an easy baby to bring along to work because he just sat so quietly. Everyone would say to me, 'Wow, he's so well-behaved.' But looking back, it was because of his conditions, which I obviously didn't know the full extent of at the time. I was getting busier and busier with jobs, and I ended up admitting that I needed some help if I was going to carry on with my career. I told my mum I didn't really want to leave him with a child minder, so she gave up her job and looked after Harvey for me when I needed it. I told her to tell me roughly what she wanted a month and I'd pay her to do it. Dwight gave her money for this in the beginning, too. It was a big thing to ask of her because it was such a huge lifestyle change for her.

My mum had a good job in the City. She'd be on the 7.08am train every morning, and then she wouldn't get home until about 7pm in the evening. She was a real grafter. My mum has always done well. She used to train at the same place as former competitive swimmer Sharron Davies and almost made the Olympic swim team. How interesting is that?

My mum was the one who got me into swimming. I used to swim for Sussex when I was younger and I trained three or four times a week. One time I was at training, and while I was swimming, it suddenly felt like my body became paralysed. I felt like I was being dragged under the water and I was going to drown. I was holding on to the rope and just screaming out for help. The lifeguard had to dive in and rescue me. From then, I started to have panic attacks, and I would have recurring nightmares about drowning. I was about 15 at the time. I couldn't swim in open water for years after that. It was such a shame because I was really into swimming, but the whole thing just shook me to my core.

I haven't had a panic attack for years, but water is still a trigger point for me. If I go on holiday, I can go in the pool or the sea and I'm a really good swimmer. But if someone was to push me in the pool unexpectedly, I'd freak out. So my family and friends know not to do that.

Mum has always been a very determined woman – and she definitely passed that on to me. I've been brought up in a family unit where we were told that you work hard and pay for the things you want. Even when there was a recession and my family was struggling, they still went to work and did everything they could for us. I come from a normal, working-class background, so I'm very proud of the business woman I've become.

I guess my mum saw helping out with Harvey as a new challenge for her. I didn't take the piss with it. It wasn't like I'd ask her to babysit because I was going out on a bender with my mates. It was only when I needed her when I was working. She still had her own life as well, but she did help me out a lot. Even to this day, she's so heavily involved in Harvey's life. He adores his nanny. Although she does drive me up the wall about him! She's always nagging me – asking if I've read emails and filled out forms. I'm like, 'Alright, Mum. Calm down!' She's so on top of things. My mum has been a backbone for me and Harvey. She's always in the know about his paperwork and appointments. In fact, if it wasn't for my mum, there's so much that wouldn't have been in place for Harvey.

Even though I was very hands-on throughout his childhood, a lot of it was all thanks to my mum. She really helped Harvey excel from a young age. She encouraged him with drawing, swimming, music – all the things children love. She's been there through everything with Harvey, and I think that's why they have such a special bond.

There have definitely been moments when my mum found it stressful taking on the role of Harvey's carer while I worked. I think one of those times was when I left her with him for two weeks to do *I'm A Celebrity... Get Me Out Of Here!*

I'd actually been asked to take part in the 2003 series, but I turned it down as Harvey was way too young for me to leave him. Imagine if I'd done it? My life would be completely different now. I wouldn't have my beautiful kids Junior and Princess for one. It's funny how things work out, isn't it?

When I was offered the show again in 2004, Harvey was two and I was still very hesitant. 'What shall I do?' I asked my mum. I really didn't like the thought of leaving Harvey – especially not for such a long period of time. I know I went to America to do my *Playboy* shoot, but Harvey was there with me, so it was different. My mum knew I felt nervous about leaving him at home, but she didn't want me to miss out again, so she said she'd come over with me and bring him with her.

There we were – all three of us going to Australia. Harvey was so good on the plane. It wasn't his first time on a long-haul flight as we'd also done our trip to America. I was going into the unknown, but I was excited. My mum and Harv were staying in the famous Versace hotel where the rest of the families stay, and I knew that everything was going to be fine.

The morning before I went into the jungle, I was kissing Harvey loads and thinking about how much I was going to miss him. But I also knew it was going to be a bit of an escape for me. I love Harvey and I love being his mum, but there's no denying that it's full-on and very hard work. The time in the jungle would be a chance to get some actual 'me time'. I would only have to worry about myself, no one else.

Well, actually, that's not entirely true, because I was constantly worrying about my campmates. I was basically doing the challenges every day, thanks to the public voting for me. There was so much pressure on me to get them food, because everyone was so hungry. So it wasn't exactly the relaxing trip to the jungle I had imagined in my head! And don't even get me started on the Bushtucker Trials that involved swimming. They terrified me after the panic attack I had in the water when I was 15.

Don't get me wrong, I missed Harvey loads when I was there. But I don't understand these people who have children and do these types of shows and just spend every day crying over them. You know you're only going to be in there a maximum of three weeks. Why do they fucking cry?! It winds me up.

You know exactly what you're signing up for – and you're getting paid to do it. It's usually a decent fee, too! I was there to do a TV programme and I just got on with it. My luxury item on the show was a photo of Harvey, so that helped a lot. Also, when you're in there, the excitement of getting out drives you and gets you through the days. And of course you talk about your kids with everyone else to keep the spirits up in camp.

Obviously, I met my first husband Peter Andre when

I was in the jungle. I had a couple of relationships when Harvey was a baby, and I was with a guy called Scott Sullivan at the time. But you know me, there's always some drama. I'd actually split up with him just before I did the show. So it wasn't just like I'd bunny hopped to another man when I got with Pete. And then Scott went to the lowest of the low and got with Jodie Marsh.

When I first got with Scott, Dwight had actually just proposed to me. We weren't together, but he kept telling my mum how much he loved me and missed me. He definitely had a funny way of showing it! But it was too late. I didn't love him. I couldn't forgive him for how he abandoned and betrayed me – and Harvey. Of course, in an ideal world I would have liked to have been with the father of my child, but life doesn't always work out like that.

While I'd had some short-lived romances, something that had always crossed my mind, like any young single mum, was, 'Who is going to ever want me?' I kept thinking, 'Will I ever find someone who can accept me and my child?' And because Harvey was born blind, I used to think that people might assume it was genetic and they might be worried about having a baby with me. 'What if they think all my kids will be disabled?' All these things constantly went through my head and it really did affect me mentally. And on top of that, I used to get vile racist abuse about having a mixed-race baby. But those people are small-minded idiots and aren't worth my time.

I can't remember the ins and outs exactly, but I told Pete all about Harvey while we were on the show – and he seemed really accepting. I don't need to go into all the details about our relationship, as it's well-documented, but when we came out of the jungle, me and Harvey went everywhere with Pete.

It was always just the three of us. Pete bonded with Harvey instantly. Family life with a disabled child is always going to be different, and Pete handled it really well. We'd be on the road together when Pete was touring and we had some really fun times. We were a proper little family unit, and I was so happy. I look back on that time with nothing but fond memories.

I don't know if any other mum can relate to this when they get into a new relationship, but you have a strong sense of protection over your child. So in the beginning, I never asked Pete to look after Harvey because I felt like he was my responsibility.

Pete was great with him, but I just felt like he was mine and I wanted to do everything for him. I felt guilty if I ever left him with Pete. But obviously Pete and I became serious and during the years I was with him, he did look after Harvey and they had an amazing relationship. Harvey called him 'Dad' because that's what he was. He didn't know any different as he was brought up with him.

The whole jungle experience was a complete whirlwind and once we were settled back home, I started to compare Harvey to other kids – and that's when I realised that something else was going on.

Five

ONE OF A KIND

A school friend of mine had a baby a few months before I had Harvey, and I would always look at her child and compare their progression. Her baby could walk around, see things, read books, and Harvey couldn't do any of that. He was just so different from any other child, and he wasn't reaching his milestones.

Harvey was obsessed with cuddling me. I know all children love their mum's cuddles, but this was different. It was to the extreme. And now I know it's because it must have been a comfort thing for him. I'll never forget the first time he cuddled me. And I mean properly cuddled me. It took Harvey years before he started wanting hugs. Before that, I would ask him for a hug and he'd give me one, but he started asking me for a hug because he *actually* wanted one. The fact he wanted my affection was such a heartwarming moment for me.

Harvey's 19 now and he still loves his mummy's cuddles. I don't blame him, I still love my mum's cuddles, too. It's just a mum's touch, isn't it? They make everything better. He must ask me about ten times a day for cuddles and kisses. It will never get annoying – I love every minute of it.

I also noticed that Harvey didn't ever try to crawl. It breaks my heart to think what he must have been going through as a baby. I suppose he didn't crawl because he couldn't see and there was nothing for him to crawl to. He just never moved, and I had to carry him everywhere. Not that I ever went to the gym, but I certainly didn't need to when I had Harvey. My God, he was heavy. It used to cause me so much back pain. And no, it wasn't because of my massive boobs!

It got to the point where I physically couldn't lift him any more, and he even became too big for his buggy. I ended up buying him a Maclaren buggy, which was designed specifically for disabled children. I've always tried to keep Harvey's life as normal as possible, and I didn't want people staring at him in his buggy, but it was a lifesaver. It was so much easier to push him around, and he was happy in it – and that's all that matters. But eventually he grew out of that, too. That's when I got him a wheelchair.

I was really reluctant about the idea, but I knew he needed one. I got one made especially for him so it was as comfortable as possible – and he didn't seem to mind it. He used to call it his 'black chair'. He didn't walk until he was about four, but he still needed his wheelchair for a couple of years after that because he wasn't confident on his feet. If he ever fell over, it was heartbreaking because it was so difficult to pick him up. If we went somewhere out of his comfort zone, he'd panic and ask for his black chair. I think he felt safe in it. Even though I knew he could walk, I felt better about him being in the wheelchair.

I became very concerned about his weight. When he was three, he weighed five-and-a-half stone. I couldn't understand why. He wasn't overeating, but if he had the choice, he would have just ate and ate until he was sick. I had to make sure I was strict about it. That's because of his Prader-Willi syndrome – a key feature is that they feel a constant sense of hunger. But we didn't know that at the time. He didn't get diagnosed with that until he was a teenager.

Although he was constantly hungry, it got to a point where he'd only eat potato smiley faces and mini kievs – he refused anything else. Even if I got a big chicken kiev and chopped it up into smaller pieces, he wouldn't eat it as he knew that it wasn't the same shape and texture as the mini ones. He's so sensitive to the way things feel. If it didn't feel right, he didn't want it.

I was worried that he wasn't getting the nutrients he needed. I couldn't give him vitamin tablets either, because he wouldn't swallow them, so I was at my wits' end. I ended up taking him to the doctor's, and he spent six weeks in Great Ormond Street while they tried to help with his diet. When they eventually got him onto other foods, he ate a lot of toast. But even with that, he had to have it cut neatly into four triangles. If it wasn't, he'd go absolutely mad.

I used to really struggle with his clothes. Even when he was just one year old, I'd have to buy him clothes that were for children aged five. But even though they fit his body, they'd be too long in the arms and legs. So in the end, I just used to make clothes for him myself with my sewing machine. Yes, you read that right – a sewing machine. Believe it or not, I own three sewing machines and it's a bit of a secret skill of mine. I've made all sorts of different things.

I've made my own curtains in previous houses, I've made my own cushions and I've even customised my own clothes. So to make Harvey's clothes, I got myself a simple pattern, cut out the templates of the size that I needed and then just used the same pattern on different fabrics. I made him lots of trousers and tops because I could never find decent clothes for him. Even now, it's hard to find trendy outfits for him as he's a size 6XL.

There are people out there who have children with special needs and they dress them really awfully. A lot of the time it's because there are no alternatives available. They should be able to dress like other kids their age, so it's always been a mission to find clothes for Harvey. If I go to a high-street shop, there's so many things I'd love to put him in, but they just don't have his size. I wish these shops would bring out a range for bigger people, because it is harder for them. Even buying underpants is a nightmare. You'd think that would be easy, but I can never find pants big enough.

Harvey now actually has his very own range with Uptheir clothing – a brand founded by a man called Ben, who has autism. Ben came to me about working with Harvey after I voiced how difficult it was to find good clothes for him. The range includes basketball vests, shorts, T-shirts, tracksuit bottoms and hoodies. It goes up to a size 8XL – and I think other companies should follow suit with that. Just because you need a bigger size, doesn't mean you can't be trendy.

Along with his weight issues, Harvey wasn't speaking either. He'd just sit there and make noises if he wanted something. I knew that he had septo-optic dysplasia and diabetes insipidus, but I was worried about the fact he wasn't talking. As he got older, at around five or six, I used to ask him things and he'd just say 'sss' instead of 'yes'. And that was about as advanced as his vocabulary was. It's so weird when I look back now, but that's how we communicated. I became more and more worried, so I took him to a speech therapist to try and get him to talk. We also had a speech therapist come round to our house, and they'd bring sensory things to try and engage Harvey. It could be something simple like a water bottle filled with beads. He loved things like that. He also loved bubble tubes with LED lights – and he still does now.

If I'd have known that Harvey was going to be blind and have some of his complex needs while I was pregnant, it would have swayed my decision and I would have gone through with the abortion. I've said that so many times before, and I know it sounds so harsh, but it's because I wouldn't have known what to do or how to cope. And I would have been frightened, especially being on my own.

But obviously, and thank goodness, I didn't know, so I was forced to deal with it when it happened. And when you're thrown into the unknown, I think you just cope with it differently. Knowing what I know now, it's such a scary thought to think I nearly lost Harvey three times by having an abortion. The thought of not having him in my life absolutely destroys me.

When we knew something was wrong with Harvey, I didn't think, 'I don't want him.' It was actually the complete opposite. I felt more love and protection than I could ever have imagined. It's weird because I sit here now and think that I would easily have another baby if it was like Harvey. I would even like to adopt a child with disabilities in the future.

But I haven't always felt that way. When I fell pregnant with Junior, I felt so much dread inside. The whole time I was just thinking, 'Will this baby have the same condition as Harvey?' I felt traumatised. And I'm not going to lie, I secretly wanted to have another boy. It's because at that time, I wanted to experience having a baby boy that didn't have any disabilities – even though at this point, Harvey hadn't even been diagnosed with half of his disabilities.

We all just presume that when we have a baby it's going to be healthy. I don't care what anyone says, you do. The fact I could have had a disabled child never even crossed my mind. I do often think about what Harvey would be like if he didn't have his conditions. But I wouldn't change him for the world.

I felt like I'd failed because I'd produced a baby that was like Harvey. Even though technically it was two people that had produced him. But it's no one's fault. I've gone on to have four more kids who are healthy, and Dwight has gone on to have another healthy child, too. I think another reason why Dwight doesn't see Harvey is because he can't handle the fact he has disabilities. You have to be a certain type of person to be able to deal with it. By the way, I just want to point out that I'm not intentionally trying to make constant digs at Dwight throughout this book, but he is Harvey's dad and I think I have every right to explain the absence of my child's dad.

I ended up finding out the sex again when I was pregnant with Junior. Like the first time, I was impatient and couldn't stand the thought of the doctor knowing when I didn't. I was absolutely over the moon to be having another boy. I didn't even try to hide my excitement. When Junior was born, I just remember pleading and praying that he would be fine and that there'd be nothing wrong with him. I'd constantly look at Junior's eyes and think, 'Is he looking at me? Can he see?' I felt constant panic. I did with all the children – the worry never got any easier.

I used to dread the health visitor appointments after what happened with Harvey. I was *so* relieved the moment I got told Junior could see. To everyone who judged me and blamed me for the way Harvey was, I felt like saying, 'Fuck you all.'

It's funny because I was so happy and grateful that Junior was fine, but I still suffered really badly with postnatal depression. It just goes to show that it can affect anyone.

If anything, you'd think that I would have experienced that with Harvey. But actually, when I've spoken to other mums who have children with disabilities, none of them had postnatal depression, from what I know of. I guess I just had to get on with things with Harvey. I didn't have a choice. Postnatal depression was one of the hardest things I've been through. I just felt so lost and confused. Getting told Harvey was blind was obviously horrendous, but I was able to cope with it because I was well and I could be strong.

I didn't understand why I couldn't bond with Junior. I had everything I wanted, so it was hard to understand why I was feeling so low. I felt that instant connection with Harvey and I showered him with love, and I knew I loved Junior equally as much, but I just thought, 'Why isn't it the same this time?' Obviously now I know it's because I was so ill. I just felt completely out of control. It took me over two years to recover from it – and I still feel guilty about it now.

Even though I was battling with depression, I still had Harvey's health to think about. We were regularly in contact with Dr Dattani – we still are now. Not long after I had Junior, Harvey was put on tablets after being diagnosed with an underactive thyroid, which is why his weight gain had started. Getting that diagnosis finally gave us the answer as to why he was so much bigger than any other child his age. His weight was putting a severe strain on his heart and lungs, which was potentially fatal, so it was such a relief that he was getting some help for it.

Dr Dattani explained that the hormones your thyroid gland releases help to regulate your metabolism. So with an underactive thyroid, it makes less hormones, meaning your metabolism slows down and you won't burn off calories as quickly. People judged me for Harvey's weight. They must have thought, 'What the hell is she feeding him? Why is she letting her child get so fat?' To be honest, I thought I'd just produced a big baby, so it was nice to know there was a scientific reason behind it.

We spent a lot of time at Great Ormond Street. It became our second home. Harvey gets recognised every time we're there. But it doesn't bother me at all if other parents come up to us, because I know what situation they're in and they know what situation I'm in. There's something nice and comforting about that place. Even though it's a hospital for really ill children, it feels like you're not alone when you're there.

When you walk around the hospital, you see children of all different ages, from all different places, with all different illnesses. It's sad, but you look at the other parents, and they look at you, and everyone kind of gives each other a little smile. There's a feeling of mutual respect. It's as if we all understand what we're going through and we're in it together. When you go to the canteen, you mingle with other parents. It's just nice to be able to talk about what you're going through with your child and to know that you're not alone.

Yes, we might all be in there for different reasons, but ultimately, we're going through the same stress and uncertainty. You know that everyone there has been referred and their health issue is serious. It's not just something a local doctor can solve. Sometimes when you go to your local doctor's surgery and you're sitting in the waiting room, you look around and wonder why people are there. Unless that's just me being a nosey cow! If someone looks perfectly okay, I think to myself, 'Do you really need a doctor?' I know that's quite judgemental of me. But when you go to Great Ormond Street, it's so different.

Every time we're there, I stay over with Harvey. Most parents are offered that because we don't want to leave our children. I have my own bed in the room with him. It's actually really nice. It's much nicer than a Premier Inn! And Harvey absolutely loves staying there.

He's been on the same ward with the same nurses since he was a baby, so it's a really familiar environment for him. There used to be a nurse there called Sinead, and she was brilliant. She really clicked with Harvey, which is hard to find, so she ended up coming to work for me alongside her full-time job. My mum was still looking after Harvey, but we could do with an extra pair of hands.

Sinead was a workaholic. She was a bit like me in that sense! She'd come from her shift at the hospital straight to our house to see Harvey. I'm actually still in contact with her to this day. She came on a lot of family trips with us and she supported me emotionally. She came to America when I did my last reality show with Pete. She was with me through all the shit – and I respect her a lot.

The only reason she stopped working for me is because I ended up moving to Brighton and it was too far for her to travel every day. Harvey still speaks about her now. He remembers all the things he did with her. It just goes to show that even though he couldn't communicate verbally, he was like a sponge and took everything in.

His memory is incredible. When I look back, it must have been hard for him. I'm sure there were times he wanted to say how he was feeling emotionally. Harvey has definitely seen a lot of things that have gone on in my life and heard some hard conversations. But one thing I've always tried to avoid is having any kind of arguments in front of my children. I want it to be a happy home, and I always want to make them feel loved and safe.

That's been tough at times, especially when I've gone through break-ups and other difficult situations. But I think that just shows my resilience. I've been through a lot of shit, probably more than the average person, but I have the strength and willpower to carry on through life's troubles – and Harvey does, too. He's one of a kind.

Six

CHALLENGING BEHAVIOUR

If I had a pound for every TV Harvey has smashed, every wall he's kicked in and every iPad he's broken, I'd be a *very* rich woman. Harvey has many complex needs, but it's his autism that causes his difficult behaviour.

I took him for so many tests when he was younger, and when he was four, that's when we got the diagnosis that he's autistic. With every diagnosis he's received over the years, it doesn't get any easier. It's heartbreaking having to add yet another thing to his long list of problems, but in the same sense, it's also a relief to get an answer. I'm a very matter-of-fact kind of person, so I can deal with things head-on once I know the reason behind a situation.

I had to be really persistent with the doctors, though. If you know anyone who has autism, you'll know that getting a diagnosis can be really difficult. It's because there's no medical test that can detect it. You can't just have an MRI scan or a blood test like you would with other conditions. It's all to do with the person's developmental history and behaviour – and that can be quite hard to measure.

The appointments we used to go to were usually around half-an-hour long. I could sit there as much as I liked telling the doctors what Harvey does at home and how challenging it can be. But on some occasions, he'd sit there looking all sweet and innocent and they'd think I was nuts. It's typical, isn't it? You're like, 'This child is a nightmare. Please believe me!' It's like he was putting on his best behaviour in front of the doctors and making his mum look like a liar!

But there were times we'd be sitting in the room with the doctors and everything was fine, and then suddenly, he'd start flipping the desks and throwing chairs across the room. Of course I hated seeing him like that, but it was a relief to know the doctors didn't think I was just some crazy woman making the whole thing up.

Once we knew he had autism, the doctors recommended some sensory toys that could be beneficial for him, which really helped. I spent quite a lot of money doing up his bedroom and making it like a sensory room.

I was in a fortunate situation where I could afford it, and Harvey was very lucky in that sense. But I felt guilty knowing that not every child could have that. Harvey's bedroom was even better than some of the professional facilities I had visited.

I never realised just how much things would cost. Even getting a wheelchair is really expensive. Not only is it expensive to cater to a disabled child's needs, it can also be really hard to get access to things. It's just small things you wouldn't even think about. For example, there was a period when I couldn't find any nappies for Harvey because he was too big to fit into the ones they sold in the shops, so the NHS had to deliver free adult-size nappies for us.

If you have an autistic child, but you haven't got the money to spare, here are a few sensory things I can guarantee they will like. You don't have to spend a fortune as they usually like things to be simple. Well, that's certainly the case for Harvey.

Lights – especially Christmas tree lights and torches. Harvey absolutely loves them both. I've been in the public eye since before Harvey was born, so he's used to the paparazzi and the cameras flashing. Sometimes he'll say, 'Leave Mummy alone.' But when he's posing for a picture, he loves the flashing light and he smiles for the camera. If you say, 'Smile, Harv,' he'll open his mouth and eyes really wide. Another thing Harvey loves is when it's thundering and lightning. It's weird because you'd think he would hate the loud noise of it, but he absolutely loves it and gets really excited when he knows a storm is coming.

Harvey also loves home-made toys. I used to fill up a plastic bottle halfway with water and just let him hold it and shake it around. Even the sound and feel of water in a bottle is sensory for them. Or I'd get some buttons from old clothes and put them in an empty bottle so that it became like a maraca for him. You really don't have to complicate it.

Even if you've got a bit of rope, you can just attach different objects onto it with pegs – as long as it's something colourful that they can see and touch. I used to just use socks. What you might think is simple and easy, is completely different in an autistic child's world.

If you close your eyes and imagine the sound, touch and texture of each object I just suggested, you will understand what I'm saying. Even walking on grass or sand bare foot can be sensory for them – although Harvey hates that! It's all about textures, shapes and colours for them. I could go on and on. Maybe I should also write a book about sensory objects!

Along with making his room sensory, I also had to have it all padded out for him so that when he kicked off he didn't hurt himself. The walls in his room were padded plastic because he used to throw himself back violently and find the nearest object and chuck it. Of course I didn't want him to live like that. I wanted to try and keep things as normal as possible, but I just had to think of his safety. He used to throw his toys a lot and at one point, I thought about making sure he only had soft toys so that he didn't hurt himself or anyone around him. But because of his sensory needs, there weren't many soft toys that were educational for him.

Another reason he needed plastic walls is because Harvey went through a stage of smearing, which is common with autism. There are different reasons as to why it might happen, but it's usually a sensory issue. It lasted a couple of years and he would smear his poo everywhere. So having plastic walls made it easier to clean as I could just wipe it down.

I don't miss that at all. It used to be *horrific*. As you can imagine, it smells. It's not a nice job to clean up. No one else can help you either because you can't expect anyone else to clean your child's poo – you've just got to get on with it. It doesn't matter if you're ill, you have to do it.

As I mentioned, I was doing a lot of nightclub appearances at the time, which was a really good money earner for me back then. So sometimes I'd wake up with a stinking hangover – pardon the pun – to poo all over the house. Whether you like it or not, you have to get on with it. I never complained, but I did often feel envious of my friends who could lie on the sofa and nurse a hangover while their child just played quietly around them. When you have a child like Harvey you don't have time to be hungover. I learnt that very quickly! I was very happy to see the back of that stage.

Harvey wasn't toilet trained until he was about six, and he still experiences a few incontinence problems today. I'm constantly having to wash his bed as he wets it a lot. It's because he has diabetes insipidus. He's on medication to help, but his body can't regulate fluids so accidents do happen.

It's a never-ending laundry pile – the washing machine is always on. Harvey keeps the electricity bill up, that's for sure. Sometimes he'll go through a phase of bedwetting more often than usual, and that's when I know his medication needs adjusting. I've tried waterproof bedding for Harvey to keep him clean and hygienic. I spent a fortune buying waterproof pillows, waterproof sheets and a waterproof duvet, but to be honest, I don't think it's worth it.

He's a 26 stone man wetting the bed – so nothing stays waterproof for long. And just because it's waterproof, it doesn't mean you can just leave it. It can give you a nasty rash and I'm sure it's very uncomfortable, so I ended up just having to change the sheets constantly anyway.

Sometimes he'll forget to go to the toilet, or he'll have an accident if he gets excited. I've taken him on a roller-coaster before (he's such an adrenaline junkie!) and he's come off completely soaking because of the excitement. And there've been incidents when we've gone shopping and he hasn't told me he needed to go to the toilet, so he's wet himself. People really stare at him as well. I feel like saying, 'Yes. I know he's wet himself. Mind your own business!' I don't have to explain myself to anyone. It's not like I can just drive all the way back home and get him changed. These things happen. So if we're going to a public place like a shopping centre or an airport, I tend to put him in pull-ups just so that we don't have an accident.

But the only trouble is, if Harvey knows he's wearing a pull-up, he won't tell me he needs to go and he'll just end up wetting himself because he knows that he can. It's a no-win situation. It's like toilet training all over again! He's also ruined a few sofas because of accidents over the years. I'm very relaxed about it – I'm just so used to Harvey damaging things now.

Harvey doesn't really understand what hygiene is, so I still have to help him shower. I get my gloves on and wash him because he can't do it properly himself. Some days he'll get in the shower and he'll say, 'Mum, I've showered myself.' And I think, 'Harv, you still stink!' He can't help it. Because he's bigger, he sweats more. I make sure he puts on loads of deodorant before we leave the house. Getting him washed really can be a military task. Some days he loves me washing his hair, and then other days he hates it. Some days he will happily brush his teeth, other days he'll kick off about it. The last time we went to the dentist, he was told he needs to start brushing his teeth a bit more. They gave him a green toothbrush to try and persuade him to do it and make it a bit more enjoyable. He promised them that he would, but we'll see how long that lasts! He's actually really well-behaved at the dentist. The staff are really good with him. He also loves having his hair cut. He's been going to the same barber for years now – and they trim his beard for him, too.

Every small thing can be a struggle – it just depends what mood he's in. There hasn't been one day where it's all been smooth sailing for us. I've never, ever experienced that. I can't imagine having a cool, calm and collected day with Harvey. But I wouldn't have it any other way.

When he kicks off, that's when he becomes destructive. You'd think Harvey was Greek by the amount of things he smashes. I used to put rubber pads on the corners of sharp things in the house, which you can just buy in a supermarket, to stop him from hurting himself. And I'd have Perspex TV screen protectors because he used to smash up the TVs.

In fact, he still does that now. It's just become a regular

thing that I'm used to because it's been happening for years. Harvey smashing up a TV is just part of the daily routine in our house. I soon realised that even if I had a Perspex protector on, he would just keep smashing the TV until he knew that he'd ruined it. So now, I've actually found a local shop that sells cheap TVs because it's just easier to keep buying new ones. I'm there so often that I probably pay the sales assistants' weekly salaries in one day!

When Harvey is in that rage, he has to follow it through because of the frustration that he feels. He has to know that what he's hitting is getting damaged, otherwise he'll keep going for it. He'll do everything in his power until something is ruined. He kicks, pulls and punches – and there's no stopping him. I've asked him before how he feels when he's in a rage, but he can't explain it to me.

This is a bit of a shit example, but the only thing I can compare it to is if you caught your partner in bed with someone else. You want to go crazy and you're not satisfied until all your anger is out. I suppose that's what Harvey feels like when he gets annoyed. He has to let some steam off. Sometimes, you think he's calmed down, but I can tell by his eyes and mannerisms that he's not out of the rage yet. I have to stick with him and calm him down because if I don't, I know he'll just go for something else and start kicking off again. You just have to let him go through it. And then afterwards he says, 'Sorry, Mum.'

At one point, I had to screw all the furniture down in his room, like the side cabinets, because he tried to lift it all up and throw it. Now he's older, he's much stronger. I got him his own house earlier this year as it just got to the point where he needed his own space. His house is in Essex and it's only over the road from me, so I can be close to him.

Harvey really likes to have a bit of peace and quiet and I thought it would be good for him to get used to having his own space ahead of him going to college. He likes his own company and he talks to himself a lot. Sometimes I'll hear him having a full-blown conversation and I'm like, 'Harvey, who the hell are you talking to?' There's also been times where people think I'm in the house, when I'm not, because he's mimicking me. If you ask him to mimic people, he can do it with ease. I have an Irish friend and he can do an impression of her accent brilliantly.

There are so many sayings Harvey and I both have. We say, 'I love it!' all the time. And we say, 'That's brilliant!' It's got to the point where I don't know whether he's got the sayings from me, or if I've got them from him. But he does copy me a lot. Sometimes he gets up from the sofa and he'll say, 'Oh, my back!' or he'll say, 'I'm exhausted!' He definitely gets that from me. We're like two peas in a pod.

Harvey's house is completely smashed up – there are holes in all the walls. But I just have to leave them there because as soon as I spend money and get them fixed, there's a huge hole there again within a week. There's no point replacing anything that's damaged until he moves out.

He recently pulled a solid oak wardrobe off the hinges and threw it against the wall, which made a massive dent. I have no idea how he managed that. It's like he has superhuman strength. I call him The Incredible Hulk. One minute he's my sweet and innocent Harvey Bear, and the next he's on a rampage! Also, just a quick message for any builders out there who are working on new houses. Just a bit of advice – you need to stop using cheap plaster. Harvey can easily put holes in the walls. Thankfully, my house was built in the 19th century and it's solid brick, so he can't ruin the walls there. I've honestly spent thousands on plastering. I think I need to set up my own plastering company at this point. I'm quite good at DIY, so surely filling holes can't be too hard.

It's totally unpredictable when Harvey kicks off. I always have to be on high alert. He's had different trigger points throughout his life. Cutlery used to be a huge trigger for him. It was so bad that we used to have special drawers at home so that he couldn't hear the sound of the knives and forks clashing against each other. When he was younger, I couldn't even take him to restaurants. I'd be persistent and try because I never wanted to leave him out, but it was a constant nightmare. Even the noise of a fork being put on the table would set him off. The next thing you know the whole table would be up in the air. It sounds unbelievable now when I look back, but that was the reality of what I dealt with.

It's crazy to think that such a young person could have so much power and strength. He ruled the roost then and he still does now. We call him the king of the house. He does live like a king. I know he has it tough, but he'll never have to worry about the things we worry about in life, like paying bills. So he has a nice life in that sense.

Lights used to be a big thing for Harvey as well. If you turned a light on in the house without telling him you were going to, he'd make you go back and turn it off. And then you'd have to wait until he told you to turn it on. Also, if we were ever in the car, he'd have to say 'click' before we could put his seatbelt on. If not, there would be uproar. God, it's exhausting even thinking about it!

Now, it's doors banging that trigger him, which it has been for years. If we go to a restaurant, we can't sit near the kitchen because the door constantly swings open and shut. I have to warn Harvey that it's going to open and close about 100 times, and I have to count out loud with him every time it does until we leave. Or I have to ask the staff at the restaurant to put something on the door to stop it from banging. They look at me as if I'm crazy, but when they see Harvey's reaction, they soon realise why I'm asking.

It's like walking on eggshells with Harv, but I've become used to it as that's his world and I understand his world. Some people who meet him might say he's spoiled and controlling, but he's not. It's just part of his autism. Harvey wouldn't even know how to be a spoiled brat if he tried. He just knows what he wants and what he doesn't want. He's very clever and he can suss out the situation to manipulate what he wants.

He wears ear defenders to help with his fear of doors and loud noises, but sometimes they don't work because his ears are so sensitive that he can just hear everything. I'm always just waiting for someone to bang a door or make a loud sudden noise, as I know it'll make him jump and he'll react by throwing something across the room.

Harvey's favourite saying is, 'Mind the door please!' And it bloody winds me up. He can be fast asleep in bed, snoring his head off, but if he hears someone opening the door, he'll wake up and shout it out. Even when I'm not with Harvey, I've found myself saying to people, 'Mind the door please!' I've even started to annoy myself.

When we go to other people's houses, I have to warn them not to bang the door. But then again, Harvey is not welcome around many houses. People might not say outright that he isn't welcome, but I can just tell by the way they respond when I tell them I'm with Harvey. I take the hint that they don't want him there, so I've learnt which houses he's generally wanted at.

I do actually find it insulting because at the end of the day, he's a human being and it's not his fault he's like this. To be honest, there are other kids who are fully able and they're actually worse than Harvey. Sometimes people bring their children to mine and they get all the toys out, go into my cupboards and eat everything in the house. I think that's rude. In fact, I think that's worse. Most of the time, Harvey won't do anything anyway. When he's in a good mood, he just sits nice and quietly on his iPad.

Don't get me wrong, I find it very hard when he's kicking off. But sometimes he'll just burst into tears – and I actually think I find that harder than dealing with his tantrums. Seeing a 19-year-old with his bottom lip wobbling and tears streaming down his face over a door banging is heartbreaking as a mum. He tries to stop himself from crying, but then he just bursts into tears. You can't help but feel sorry for him – he's like a big baby.

Noises make him jump so much because he can't see what's going on. If you hear something, you can just look around to see what it was, but Harvey can't do that, so he goes into a shock and gets upset. Harvey has peripheral vision loss, which means he can only see what's straight in front of him – and even that is very blurry. Everything else around him is just darkness. So when he looks straight ahead, he can't see up and down or to the sides.

Going out in public is a *nightmare*. I feel like I'm constantly clearing up after him and I fork out a lot of money to repair things he's smashed up. Fortunately, I know that if he breaks something, I can pay for it, but it does end up costing me a lot of money. It's not ideal. I honestly don't know how families who can't afford to replace things cope.

I once took a trip to the nail salon and brought Harvey along with me because he loves getting his own manicure. But that nail appointment ended up costing me £460. Our nails looked nice, but bloody hell, not for that price! A Justin Timberlake music video was playing on the TV and Harvey simply didn't like it, so he picked the nearest thing up, threw it at the TV and smashed it. I had to give the salon the money to replace their TV. Sometimes I do worry they'll just pocket the money, but I've been back to the salon since and they have replaced it. I won't be taking Harvey back there any time soon, that's for sure!

This is the thing with Harvey, anything can annoy him. And sometimes it's really unexpected. For example, we were once sitting in the lounge and the TV was on in the background. Harvey wasn't even watching it, but he got frustrated that whatever programme was on had finished, so he chucked the TV remote at it.

Another time, he got the hiccups while we were driving in the car. It annoyed him, so he started smashing the window. I asked him why he did that and he said, 'Because I've got hiccups.' I said, 'But look what you've done to the window,' and he replied, 'It's naughty, isn't it?' So he understands that he shouldn't do it, but he can't help it. I ended up filming the aftermath and sharing the video on Instagram to show people just how bad he can be. When he's in that rage, he's gone up to random people's cars before and just gone for their windscreen.

I can never truly relax when we're out, but I like to take him to places as I'm so determined not to keep him isolated from everything. I try to keep his life as normal as possible. But on a day out I'm always like, 'What's he going to break today?' And that's just how it is with him now. It's gotten worse as he's gotten older. I can completely understand why some parents who have got kids like Harvey, or adults like Harvey, put them in a care home. Sometimes, it's safer for them and it's safer for everyone else around them.

Even having pets isn't straightforward. We've always had dogs in our house, but he hates them. If they're barking, he'll shout, 'Shut the fuck up!' If he's kicking off,

I do worry he might pick the dog up and try to throw it, so I have to really keep an eye on him.

It's also really hard to find places that make the whole family happy when you have a disabled child. It's difficult because I feel bad for the other kids that my attention has to be with Harvey, but at the same time, he shouldn't be left out. There's not a lot of stuff out there for people who have disabilities, or for people in wheelchairs. Harvey absolutely loves theme parks. Like I said, he loves adrenaline. We do go to theme parks a lot as a family, but we have to go straight to the front of the queues because he doesn't like waiting.

People probably think it's because I'm in the public eye and I'm getting special treatment, but it's actually for Harvey. I'm more than happy to queue – I don't care at all. But it's not fair on Harvey because he gets distressed. If we had to stand in the queue, he'd be kicking off and trying to hit people. He doesn't understand why he has to wait. Also, I can't stand people taking pictures of us. It really pisses me off when people think they have a right to do that. It's a total invasion of my privacy. I know it's part and parcel of my job, but we're not in a circus. When we go somewhere like Alton Towers, we're there to enjoy the attractions. But some people seem to think we're the attraction.

Unfortunately, Harvey's weight can also stop him

from doing things he wants to do. The last time we went to a theme park, he was too big to go on a ride as the seat belt didn't fasten up. He didn't understand why and I had to tell him it's because of his belly. He recently lost two stone, which is great, but he's still very big. I try my best to make him exercise, but it's hard. It's not like he can just run for ten minutes on a treadmill. He gets out of breath very quickly. We have to do it differently with Harvey because of his medical needs. He enjoys doing a bit of boxercise, but it has to be to music that he likes. You basically just have to make it fun for him. Once he starts, he quite enjoys it, but it's actually getting him to start which is the hard part.

I think there should definitely be rides out there for people in wheelchairs. Just because someone is disabled, it doesn't mean they don't enjoy a thrill. I'm not saying the rides have to go upside down and do loops, but at least something to give them a bit of adrenaline. Perhaps that should be my next Government campaign! I feel quite strongly about it because there are so many people out there who weren't born disabled and have had an accident which has left them wheelchair-bound for life. Just because they've had an accident, doesn't mean they've stopped enjoying things like that. If I'm being totally honest, before I had Harvey, I was quite ignorant and I didn't really have a clue about disabilities and how they affect people. If I saw anyone in a wheelchair, I didn't really think anything of it. But when you live and breathe it, you see it all from a different perspective.

I was in a wheelchair myself when I broke both of my feet in 2020. I was on holiday in Turkey and I jumped off a wall. It was dark at the time and I completely misjudged how big the wall was – it ended up being a 20ft drop. I landed on my feet and completely shattered them. It makes me cringe to even think about it.

I found it incredibly difficult to look after Harvey, but I still somehow managed it. I couldn't help him when he was kicking off because I could hardly get around myself. I was still his carer, even though I needed someone to care for me. I was registered disabled and qualified for a Blue Badge. Harvey really sympathised with me and understood that I'd hurt my feet. He used to say to me, 'Be brave, Mummy.' It upset him that I was upset. That was such a difficult period in my life. I still struggle to walk now – my feet will never be the same.

Going on holiday is also a massive drama for us. Holidays are meant to be relaxing, but it can be a nightmare. Airports are the worst place for Harvey because again, it's a lot of queuing. When we do have to queue, he'll distract himself by flicking an object really close to his face. It's usually something like a clothes hanger. People probably think he's going to flick it in his face and hurt himself. But he's never done that – he knows how to do it. He used to do it all the time with things like rulers.

I always dread going through security at an airport with him as well, because you have to take your shoes off when you go through the scanner. Mind you, I should be the one dreading going through the scanner with the amount of metal in my feet now! Every single time, Harvey refuses to take his shoes off and he kicks off like crazy. I say to the staff, 'Please can he just keep his shoes on? It's just not worth it.' But they insist that he has to take them off. I know they're just doing their job – it's about security and they are right to ask of this – but at the same time, it's a massive ball-ache and it causes more harm than good. I think more people should be educated about autism.

As we used to travel a lot when he was a baby, he just became so used to being in first class on long-distance flights with flat beds. Because of his autism, he likes having a routine and he expects things to be in their set ways. So now, whenever we get on a smaller plane, like one of easyJet's or Ryanair's, he kicks off straight away because he wants to put his pyjamas on and go to sleep on a flat bed. He once said really loudly, 'Mummy, where are the beds and duvets please?' I was so embarrassed. All the other passengers definitely judged us!

I always have to warn him in advance and explain to

him that those kinds of planes don't have them. If we're going somewhere like Spain, I have to keep telling him that we're only going to be on the plane for two hours and then we can get off. But he still kicks off – and then everyone on the plane stares. It's like when you have a baby that's crying throughout the whole flight and you just know that people are getting annoyed. But it's not his fault. He can't help it.

If he's not kicking off on the plane, he spends the whole journey talking. He speaks in a very loud, clear voice and I know the whole flight can probably hear him. When the air hostess comes through with her trolley, he asks, 'What's your name? You're beautiful.' He can be a right little charmer! Whenever he speaks to a woman, he'll say, 'Hello beautiful.' Or if it's a man, he says, 'Hello handsome,' and 'Hello mate.' He definitely can identify the different genders. But he's not quite up to date with the LGBTQ+ community yet!

There have also been times where he's just refused to get off the plane once we've landed. There's one time in particular that stands out in my memory. Everyone had to get off the plane through the back door because Harvey threw himself onto the floor and wouldn't move. It was all because he wanted a pizza on the plane and they didn't have one. I sometimes have to tell him little white lies otherwise we could be there all day. I said to him, 'We need to get off now so we can get onto another plane and then you can have your pizza.' Or in similar situations, I say to him, 'If you don't calm down there will be no carrot cake.' He knows that there are consequences to his actions. Food always wins him over – and so does praise. He gets so excited if you praise him.

To calm him down, I say 'Harvey Price' in a soft, slow voice. And then I sing nursery rhymes to him. He likes *Round And Round The Garden* at the moment. It can take ages for him to calm down though, and it just depends on the day. Sometimes it can take ten minutes, other times it can take hours. Until people see what I'm like with him, they don't realise what it takes to calm him down. And it takes a lot of patience, I can tell you that!

When we finally got him off the plane and into the tunnel, he started again. He was kicking and screaming and trying to rip the phones off the walls. He was causing such a scene that the police came with guns. I was trying to explain that everything was fine and that I just needed to calm him down. He really can cause havoc!

When he kicks off like that, I can only describe it as like a helicopter on the floor. He spins around on his legs and tries to kick and smash everything in his surroundings. It's actually quite a talent. I think even Diversity would be impressed with that move.

Another thing about going on holiday is that a lot of

hotels have clothing policies for their restaurants. One time, we were staying in an all-inclusive hotel and Harvey didn't want to put a T-shirt on for breakfast. He likes being naked – that's quite a common trait with autism because they can find the feeling of clothes against their skin uncomfortable. That's why in a lot of videos I take of Harvey, you might have noticed he doesn't have his top on. He also really hates clothes with zips on them. This is another reason it's so hard to shop for him.

But anyway, back to the point. We turned up at the hotel's restaurant and Harvey was in his wheelchair, so you could quite clearly see he was disabled. The staff looked at him and said to us, 'Sorry, you can't come in if he isn't wearing a T-shirt.' I tried to explain the situation, telling them he's autistic and he'll kick off if I make him put it on. But they just wouldn't let us in. So I had to force Harvey to put his T-shirt on. And what did he do? He started smashing everything in sight and causing a complete scene in the restaurant, of course. So they eventually let him take it off again – and he was all smiley and happy.

If they'd have just let him in to start with, none of that would have happened. I get that it can be hard for people to understand, especially if you've never been around somebody with autism. But you would think they'd be a bit more compassionate. Sometimes I feel like walking around with a big sign attached to me saying, 'Harvey is autistic and these are the things he doesn't like.' I also think restaurants should have dedicated quiet areas for people with sensory needs because it's more common than you'd think.

It's really hard for us to go on all-inclusive holidays, so now we just tend to stay in villas so that we have the place to ourselves and there's nobody there to stare. There have been times before when we've been sitting around the pool and people have taken pictures of us on their phones. It really winds me up. Harvey loves playing in the pool with a bucket and he makes frog noises. He also loves taking my phone and filming himself blowing bubbles under the water because it reminds him of a bubble tube – a piece of sensory equipment. I can see why people might find him fascinating to watch, but I just find it plain rude when we're out and people just stand and stare.

I can tell people are judging me. I say to them, 'Are you alright there? Are you having a good stare?' Sometimes I just can't hold my tongue. I've got used to it now, because you have to. I actually used to carry around cards that I'd printed out and hand them to people when I saw them staring at Harvey. The cards said, 'You're obviously looking because you're interested. These are his conditions and if you want to donate to a charity that supports children like this then here are the details.' It certainly stopped people from staring. Maybe I should start doing it again.

The last time we went away, I took him to Saint Lucia for a family holiday. We had an interconnecting room and it was beautiful. But Harvey absolutely destroyed it. He put loads of holes in the walls because he kicked off almost every day. He also has a habit of picking the skin on his leg until it bleeds and then he wipes the blood on the wall and all over the bed sheets. It's a sensory thing for him. I had to tell the hotel that I'd pay for the damage – and it's not cheap.

When I'm out and about, I notice straight away if someone has autism. You're so much more aware of it when you have a child who has it. I can just tell by people's mannerisms. I don't know what it is, I just feel very in tune with it.

I went to the Isle of Wight recently and noticed a boy with his mum. He reminded me so much of Harvey and I just knew he had autism. I said to the mum, 'You've got your hands cut out for the day. Your son's got autism, hasn't he?' At first, she looked at me as if to say, 'Wow, you're rude.' But then I explained how Harvey also has autism and how similar he was. It was like a weight had been lifted off her shoulders because I just understood her situation. You have to have so much patience when you have a child with autism. It's just constant – there's no break from it. It's very stressful. It's nice when you can talk about your experiences with other people. It's rare that it happens because I don't know anyone close to me who has a child like Harvey. The children he went to school with are all from different areas, so it's difficult to stay in touch with the parents.

I've never met anyone like Harvey. I would absolutely love to, though. It can be really isolating because yes, you can talk to people who have got children with autism or ADHD or a disability, but I've never met anyone else who is exactly like Harvey. But then again, even without disabilities, everyone is different.

Harvey also suffers with anxiety. He gets it quite bad when I'm not with him. If I ask him what makes him sad, he says, 'Being away from Mummy.' It does break my heart. He also gets it if we're going somewhere new and he doesn't know what to expect. That's why he asks a lot of questions. It's like, 'Where are we going? What are we doing? How long will we be? Where are we going after that? What's for dinner later?' He likes to know exactly what's going on and once he knows the details, he starts to relax.

I also have to explain to him that after we've been out, we'll end up back at home and that makes him happy. It's just constant talking and a lot of repetitiveness with Harvey. Some people spend a couple of hours with him and say they're exhausted, so that's the kind of level I'm talking about. If I'm trying to talk to someone and I'm with Harvey, he's always interrupting and wanting my attention, so I have to stop my conversation and talk to him to stop him from kicking off. At least when he was younger I could pull him away. But now, I can't lift him up because he's almost triple my weight.

I live in the fast lane with Harvey and I always have to be one step ahead of him. He can't have many people around him and you can't keep chopping and changing things because it upsets him. When new people come into his life, it has to be a gradual process. You have to leave Harvey to work it out. But I do have one tip to get him on your side – bring carrot cake! If you bring him a cake, he'll love you forever.

I don't know why he loves carrot cake so much. He loves sweet things. He started off loving blueberry muffins, and then it turned into chocolate muffins, and now it's carrot cake. He doesn't ever want any other cake. If I give him a blueberry muffin, he says, 'No thank you, Mummy. Only carrot cake.' I'm like, 'Harvey, you were obsessed with blueberry muffins!' Now he's not interested in them at all. He can switch his opinion on things very quickly.

When you're around someone like Harv, you've got to try and understand it from their perspective and imagine how they must see things. You've got to go along with their journey because if you don't understand what they're feeling or sensing, then it's hard work. I can't just leave anyone with Harvey and expect everything to be fine and for him to get on with the day. It just wouldn't happen. That's why I've been so worried about him settling in at his new college with new surroundings and new people. Because he likes a structured routine, Harvey and new things don't always go well together.

Harvey is currently at Maudsley Hospital, where he's been going for years. It's a hospital in south London that provides mental-health services. I love going there and Harvey knows the doctors really well. They've seen him at his very worst – they've had to duck down and take cover when he's had his tantrums!

The rooms at Maudsley have whiteboards in them, which Harvey loves. The doctors know him so well now – as soon as we arrive, he's given pens so that he can draw them a picture. He draws trains or frogs and he always writes a note for the doctor alongside it. It's usually something along the lines of, 'Dear doctor, Harvey has been very good.' He always adds 'ribbit ribbit' – his favourite sound to make – and puts lots of kisses at the end. He does make me laugh.

He's very clever. Every time he sees the doctor he tells them he's going to be well-behaved from now on and that he's going to start eating healthy foods, because he knows that's exactly what they want to hear. But does Harvey ever follow that up at home? Of course not.

CHALLENGING BEHAVIOUR

Whether you've got disabilities or not, you've still got to go through puberty. So like any other teenager, Harvey has faced those challenges. I always say Harvey is currently going through the 'Kevin and Perry' stage.

As you can imagine, on top of his already difficult behaviour, it's been hard work. He's had everything that comes with puberty – the mood swings, the facial hair, the spots. I love picking his whiteheads, which Harvey absolutely hates. But our relationship is all about compromising. He loves going on trains, which I hate. We've learnt to give and take.

People see a lot of the good times we have together, and my God, we have some really good times. But Harvey is hard work and it's very draining. I rarely show the side of Harvey kicking off, because I don't feel like people need to see it – I like people to see the good side. If people saw what he's like when he kicks off, it would be disturbing to watch. People reading this who know someone with a disability will know what I mean.

But I'm not moaning about any of it. I love him to bits and I wouldn't change him for the world. Besides, life would be very boring without any challenges.

Seven

NANNY NIGHTMARES

Because of Harvey's challenging behaviour, it's always been a struggle to find a nanny who's a good fit for our family. It's hard enough to find a decent nanny in general, but Harvey doesn't click with many people and even the most qualified nannies think he's too much hard work.

I'd always looked after Harvey myself with the help of my mum, but as he got older and as our family got bigger, it became harder and harder. I love being a mum and I always have done – it's the best job in the world. But I also loved my career. I wasn't ready to take my foot off the pedal just yet. But oh my God, searching for a good nanny became a job in itself. My luck with nannies has almost been as bad as my luck with men. And that's saying something!

There was a terrible incident in 2007 when Harvey broke his nose. The aftermath was all caught on camera as we were filming our reality show *Katie & Peter: The Baby Diaries*. Our nanny at the time said that a mirror in the house had accidentally fallen on him.

Starting from the beginning, it was a bank holiday Monday and I went to Toys"R"Us with Pete because we were buying presents for Harvey's upcoming birthday. We'd really gone all out and I was so excited about what I'd bought him. I couldn't wait to see his little face light up when he opened his presents.

We were on our way back in the car when I got a phone call from an unknown number. I don't always answer numbers I don't recognise, but I had a strange feeling in my gut.

It was a man's voice. 'Hello, is that Katie?'

'Speaking,' I said.

It was a paramedic phoning to tell me there'd been an accident at home and Harvey and the nanny were injured. 'What?! What's happened?! Is Harvey okay?' I asked frantically. Junior was also at home with them and the paramedic explained that we needed to come back as soon as possible as they couldn't leave for the hospital until Junior was supervised.

Whenever Harvey has an accident or is poorly, he has to take an emergency cortisone injection. Basically, if he doesn't take it there's a danger he could go into shock and his windpipe could close up. To put it bluntly, he could die. So the first thing I did was explain to the paramedic that he needed that urgently. I tried to remain calm, but I wanted to get home as quickly as I could and we were still quite far away. Not to brag or anything, but we'd chosen to go in our new Ferrari that day. It was absolutely pissing it down and you have to drive really carefully in those cars because they can spin out of control in wet conditions. So it wasn't ideal when we were in a rush!

When we arrived home, there were two ambulances on our driveway. The nanny was in one – she looked fine but was complaining of back pain and possible concussion. And then Harvey was in the other with gas and air. He had cuts all over his little face and he was covered in blood. His nose was also really badly swollen.

When I walked into the house, there was blood all over the hallway. It was absolutely horrific! It looked like a crime scene. I had a huge glass mirror fitted on the wall – the kind that had to be properly mounted because it was so big. It was brand new as well. I'd only bought it four days before. When I asked the nanny what had happened, she explained that Harvey had been playing with his toys in the hallway. The mirror just fell on top of him and somehow flipped over, smashed into a thousand pieces and cut his nose. She said she dived in front of him to stop the mirror from fully crushing him. But I didn't really have time to question anything. My focus was on Harvey. I got into the ambulance and went to the hospital with him, while Pete stayed at home with Junior. The journey there was awful. Harvey wasn't saying anything and he wasn't moving – it was frightening to see him like that. When we got there, the nurses cleaned up Harvey's face and he started crying in agony. As a mother, seeing your child in pain and knowing there's nothing you can do has got to be the worst feeling in the world. Especially because Harvey couldn't communicate.

The nanny was discharged from the hospital pretty much straight away. She was checked over and told she was fine, but Harvey had to have stitches for the wounds on his face. He also had to have an X-ray on his nose as they suspected it could be broken. The X-ray confirmed it was – and he still has the scar across the top of his nose to this day.

He ended up having to stay in because they needed to operate on him. He had to have his nose put back into place and his cuts stitched. Harvey's nose was so bad that I actually had to show the surgeon a picture of him so that he could see what his nose was supposed to look like.

I was allowed into the operating theatre with Harvey.

He was such a brave boy. They wanted to keep him in for a couple of nights so that they could monitor him. I was absolutely exhausted. I was heavily pregnant with Princess at the time and just a few weeks away from the birth. The last place I wanted to be was in the hospital. I just wanted to take Harvey home and snuggle up in bed with him and give him lots of cuddles and kisses. But we had to do what was best for him. And if that meant staying in, then so be it.

We'd had trouble with this nanny while she was working for us in the past. She was the same nanny we had when Harvey scalded his leg in the bath on New Year's Eve in 2006 – just a few months before the mirror accident.

That was the night I genuinely thought I was going to lose Harvey – and it's a night I will never forget. The year of 2007 couldn't have started any worse. Poor Harvey really went through it that year. I genuinely felt like he had been cursed and someone out there was putting me to the test to see how much worry and stress I could take.

We were having a big pyjama party at ours to see in the New Year. I spent days getting the house ready and I'd organised for caterers to come over so we had plenty of food and drink for our guests. I really went all out for it.

During the day, I went to look at a horse I was interested in buying. Yes, you might think that New Year's Eve was a bit of a strange time to do that, especially when I was getting ready for a party, but I didn't get much free time so I took any opportunity I could. Besides, the nanny was looking after Harvey and Junior.

I got home around two hours before our guests were due to arrive, so I had plenty of time to get ready.

I was just taking my riding boots off when I heard Harvey screaming upstairs. I presumed he was just having one of his tantrums. The nanny went up to check on him, and a few minutes later she started shouting my name – I knew something was seriously wrong by the tone of her voice.

I rushed up the stairs and Harvey was laying on the bed wriggling around in agony. He had blood all over his right leg. 'He needs an ambulance!' I shouted. I was trying to stay calm, but I was horrified. I was trying to work out what had happened. His leg was full of loose skin and all his clothes were wet. I ran into the bathroom and that's when I realised he'd scalded himself.

I later found out that nobody had shut the baby gate at the bottom of the stairs and he went up without anyone noticing. He loved having a bath with me, so he'd gone into the bathroom and turned the tap on himself, obviously not knowing it was hot water, and got in it. He then somehow managed to get himself out and crawl onto the bed. It breaks my heart to know that he was on his own and no one was there to help him for those few minutes.

I quickly pulled his tracksuit trousers down, not knowing that I'd actually made it worse by doing that. Apparently you're supposed to leave the clothes on because the air on the open burn can cause even more damage. I felt so guilty. After that, I had first-aid training because I wanted to have more knowledge if I ever found myself in a situation like that again.

Harvey was screaming and I just felt helpless. I also knew that he needed his emergency injection, so it wasn't just a normal burns case. But I was in such a state there's no way I would have been able to give him the injection myself. It's so big and it's quite complicated to do. I rang 999 and told them Harvey had been burned and he needed the injection immediately. I'm not even sure how I strung a sentence together – it was all such a blur.

Waiting for the ambulance to arrive felt like hours. I think it took around half an hour for it to come, which is a long time when your child is suffering and needs urgent help. I couldn't even try and comfort and cuddle Harvey as we waited because he didn't want anyone near him. The paramedics gave Harvey his injection and then rushed him to hospital. I travelled in the ambulance with him and it was the journey from hell. Harvey just didn't seem with it at all – and I became more and more frightened. At one point, it looked like Harvey wasn't breathing. It must have only been a couple of seconds, but in those seconds, I really thought I was losing my son. I was around three months pregnant with Princess at this point, so I was also worried about what the stress would do to the baby.

We arrived at Royal Sussex Hospital and there were loads of doctors waiting for us. I had to explain to them all about Harvey's medical needs. Because of his conditions, you can't just treat him how you would anyone else. There's a lot of medication they can't give him as something could react with the tablets that he takes daily.

Normally, you'd give someone morphine for the amount of pain he was in, but he couldn't have any. So they put him on oxygen and monitored him. Harvey's leg looked awful. The burn was red raw and it looked so painful.

The party was the last thing on my mind, but I had to text everyone to tell them Harvey had been taken to hospital after a serious accident. We had so much food in the house and I didn't want it to go to waste, and some people were travelling miles so they'd already set off. I told them they were still welcome to come, but we just wouldn't be there. Instead, we were eating chocolates with the nurses as the clock turned to midnight. It's definitely not how I'd imagined I'd be spending the start of the year.

The doctors said they were unable to treat him at the

hospital because they didn't have the resources, so he was transferred straight to Chelsea And Westminster Hospital in London, where he ended up staying for about four months in the end.

I was by his side the whole time and I just kept hugging him and telling him how much I loved him. I felt so sorry for him. He didn't deserve to be going through any of this. His burn was so severe, more than I had first realised. Normally, doctors would treat it by giving him a skin graft, but his condition was too unstable because of his complex needs. They were also worried that a skin graft might not even work and then he would end up with even more wounds.

So instead, they had to scrub Harvey's burn to stop any infection and to encourage new skin to grow. They had to scrape back his skin every single day to try and repair it. Can you imagine how painful that must feel? And like I said, he couldn't have any pain relief. He couldn't speak at this point, so I can't even imagine how difficult it must have been for him not being able to communicate while someone is scraping the skin off your leg.

His screams still haunt me to this day. I had to run down the corridor to get away from it, but I could still hear him through the doors. It was the worst thing in the world. The image of his poor little face will never leave me. I remember being able to see every single tooth in his mouth because it was wide open while he was crying. It was an absolute nightmare. A frightening nightmare.

Despite everything the doctors were doing, his leg just wasn't healing. And then it became infected. It looked and smelled horrific. My poor little boy just couldn't catch a break. He was in so much pain and he was so upset, so he understandably lost his appetite. He wouldn't even eat his favourite meal of smiley faces and mini kievs! So his recovery was made even slower because he just wasn't eating and he didn't have any energy.

They had to put him on a drip to help him get his nutrients. He looked so poorly. At one point, they even thought he had pneumonia. I really started to feel like things weren't going to get any better, but then the doctors came up with a plan. They started to double the dose of Harvey's growth hormone, Genotropin, which he takes once every night. They hoped that by doing that, his body would have more strength to recover. After just one day of doubling the dose, his leg finally showed some signs of healing. I felt so relieved.

The consultant actually asked us if he could use Harvey as a case study, because they'd never had to treat a burn victim with such complex conditions before. Harvey then had to have physio to help him walk, as the skin was still repairing. They told us that if he didn't start moving, the new skin would grow in a way that would make walking difficult for him. Harvey had only just started walking properly, so it was heartbreaking to think this could set him back. It took about three months until he was able to walk again after the accident. It was a very long, slow process.

Just when I started to feel optimistic, a doctor said to me, 'You're not going to be able to discharge him, I'm afraid.' I was like, 'What do you mean?!' He'd made so much progress – I was in disbelief at what I was being told.

'You've been reported to social services,' he said. 'What?! By who?!' I was raging. It turned out a nurse at Royal Sussex Hospital had put a complaint in about me. She accused me of scalding Harvey's leg deliberately. I was so offended. How dare she!

I remember just getting on the phone to social services and giving them an earful. I told them they were a complete joke and they should be investigating real cases. I was rude to them, but I was absolutely fuming. How dare someone try and stick their nose in. The police turned up with social services at the house and we had to show them exactly what had happened and where it had happened. To be honest, I think they were embarrassed to be in the house because clearly they knew we were telling the truth. Once they could see that there was obviously nothing to be concerned about, it was left at that. In all fairness, social services were doing their job. It would have been wrong not to investigate it.

I phoned Harvey's doctors at the time and explained what had happened and how someone had called social services on me. They were shocked. If Harvey really was being neglected, those doctors would be the first to spot any signs. Without his medication daily, he would die. So how on earth could I possibly be neglecting him?! It hurt me so much.

Harvey was eventually discharged, and while it was a long recovery, he was happy to be back home. He needed a lot of extra love and attention after everything that had happened, and I hugged him a little tighter every single night. Sadly, Harvey is scarred for life, and he still picks at the damaged skin now.

It also took him months until he was able to have another bath again – he was so terrified of what had happened. And when he did have a bath, I would have to prove to him that it was cold water before he got in so that he knew there was nothing to be scared of. Thankfully, he now absolutely loves water and I don't think he has much memory from those horrible months.

Before I move on, I just want to go back to my point about social services. The thing is, anyone can report anyone. You can phone them up, make a report about someone, and it's as easy as that. People definitely have a vendetta against me. If they receive a complaint, they have to follow it up and investigate, which I understand. But it's just a waste of time that could instead be spent investigating real neglect.

When it happens, it's so embarrassing and degrading. It's such a horrible feeling to think that someone is accusing you of mistreating your child. Sadly, I've had them in and out of my life because people like to call them to cause trouble. They've been to my house a few times, and it's just laughable. They can see how well all my kids are treated. When they come to the house, they look around and look at all of the bedrooms. They can see that all my children have lovely bedrooms full of toys and books.

If I was unfit to look after my children, the first child you would look at for evidence is Harvey because of the amount of care he needs. It's just ridiculous. Even when I was mentally unwell before I went to The Priory, my kids were never affected by it. I made sure of it.

I can take a lot of shit. Say anything you like about me. You can call me a slag, you can call me talentless, you can call me a surgery freak, I really don't care. But one thing I don't like is people insinuating I'm a bad mother.

That's why I sued the *News Of The World* back in 2008. As I said earlier, it's very hard to argue against a newspaper and it's usually not worth the time or money, but I wasn't going to take this one lying down. They ran an interview with our former nanny and falsely claimed that Pete and I were bad parents who neglected our kids. It was a front page story which ran over five pages and was headlined, 'Jordan Exposed: Nanny reveals sex, rows, binges and what she's really like as a mum.'

The nanny made a lot of untrue accusations against us during the interview. I couldn't even bring myself to read the lies. I was so upset. She implied that Pete was to blame for Harvey's scalded leg – despite social services investigating the incident. She also said we were feeding Harvey a diet of junk food, which was to blame for his weight. Even though his weight is obviously because of his condition.

Usually, when a story like that comes out, the paper would come to your agent for a right of reply. But we had no warning about it and no chance to tell them it was completely made up. I got in contact with our lawyers straight away. I knew I could disprove every single claim the nanny had made. I just couldn't believe the lies that had been printed, and I wasn't going to let them get away with it. It was a really dark time. If you have kids, you can imagine how it would feel to be publicly accused of being a bad parent.

We won the case, of course, and accepted substantial damages and a public apology from the paper. We donated half of the money to the NSPCC and the Vision Charity, and we put the other half into a trust fund for the kids.

It was a stressful process to go through, but we had to clear our names. Even though it was proved that the story was all lies, it still made me feel like shit. The thing is, people do believe what they read in a paper, and I hated the thought of people believing I was a bad mum. But in the end, I just had to put it behind me. I'll never know what motivated the nanny to go to the press and do that to my family. I can only assume it was to pocket some cash.

The drama with nannies didn't stop there. And this is all before I caught Kieran having an affair with our nanny! Jacqueline Gold, the CEO of Ann Summers, phoned me up one day as she was interviewing a nanny who had put on her CV that she'd worked for me in the past.

She wanted to get a reference from me and was asking about the experience I'd had with her. We basically employed this nanny and we took her to America with us and everything, so we'd spent a lot of time with her.

But I slowly noticed that she started cloning into me. It was so freaky. It was just little things that she would copy, like she'd start having the same colour nails as me. Okay, the first time could have been a coincidence, but there wasn't just one time. She'd also start wearing the same clothes as me. It all got too much and in the end, we got rid of her because it was very weird.

I didn't really say much about her to Jacqueline – after what we'd been through in the past, I guess she wasn't *that* bad. I didn't want to be a bitch and stop someone from getting a job. Besides, copying someone isn't exactly a crime. They do say imitation is the best form of flattery!

Jacqueline was obviously impressed by her and ended up giving her the job. Anyway, the next thing I know, it came out in the press that she had tried to poison Jacqueline! There it was as headline news: 'Nanny admits poison bid on Ann Summers' Jacqueline Gold.' How mental is that?! Poor Jacqueline. I should have warned her that she was a nutcase, but I didn't think she actually *was* a nutcase. She had put screen wash in her food and was sentenced to a year in prison.

I always hired my nannies through agencies, so it wasn't like I found them on dodgy websites or anything like that. There was another one I hired who helped look after Harvey. One day, she left her work phone at ours by mistake and she kept acting really suspicious about it. You know when someone is trying really hard to be normal, but it makes them seem even more suspicious? It was like that.

She kept telling us that if the phone ever rang, we should just leave it. I kept thinking, 'What is she hiding?' So I went on her phone and saw all these videos of Harvey in the bath that she had secretly recorded and saved. We ended up calling the police. Nothing came of it, but we got rid of her straight away. After going through such a bad time, I felt more protective over Harvey than ever.

Eight

FATHER FIGURES

That overwhelming sense of protection for Harvey has never gone away. If anything, it's become greater as he's gotten older.

I've had many people in and out of my life, but the one person who has stuck with me throughout everything is Harvey – and he's the only one who nobody can take away from me.

But the sad truth is, Harvey doesn't have a dad. Even his own biological father doesn't want him. I share my other children with their dads, so in a way, it's nice to know that Harvey is always with me and I can have him 100 per cent of the time.

The split from Pete really did upset Harvey. It must

have been frustrating for him at the time because he couldn't express how he felt.

It's the same with Kieran. It's a shame as they were both brilliant with Harvey when I was with them. I can't knock them for that. Harvey might have complex needs, but I know it has really affected him because he does understand. He used to call them both 'Daddy', so of course it affects him.

Even to this day, I think it reflects in his behaviour. Just because Harvey isn't as verbal as us, it doesn't mean he doesn't have feelings and isn't aware of a situation. This is why I'm very cautious about introducing men to Harvey. I don't want Harvey to form a bond with someone only for circumstances to change and they're no longer a constant presence in his life.

When I split from Pete, he would still see Harvey. In 2009, Harvey ended up in hospital because he had a high temperature and breathing difficulties. Thankfully, he was fine, but he just needed to be monitored.

I contacted Pete because even though we weren't together, I knew he would have wanted to see him. Harvey kept calling us 'Mummy and Daddy' because he obviously didn't know what was going on between us at the time.

Our marriage might have been over, but Pete was his daddy. Harvey used to visit Pete most weekends, but because of his medical needs, he had to be accompanied by a trained nanny on any visits. Then, as time went on, I began to notice a change in Harvey. I'd say things like, 'Do you want to go see Daddy Peter today?' And he'd shout, 'No!' So then I'd be like, 'But he has a cake waiting for you.'

But he wasn't interested and he'd start kicking off. It's probably because the visits were starting to fizzle out and Harvey could sense that. When Harvey is refusing cake, that's when you know he's upset.

I wasn't going to force my son to do something he didn't want to do. Pete was good for Harvey and I'd do anything to make my son happy. But Harvey is very emotionally intelligent and he doesn't forget things that have gone on in the past.

Fair enough, Pete and Kieran weren't his biological dads, but Harvey called them both 'Daddy', and to him they were.

These days, Harvey will see them both on the odd occasion, like when I'm picking the other kids up or dropping them off. But oh my God, Harvey doesn't half make it awkward for us sometimes.

He's so funny. Whenever he sees Pete, he'll open up YouTube on his iPad and start playing the clip of us singing *A Whole New World*. Every single time, I want the ground to swallow me up. It's bad enough having to listen back to it, never mind having to listen back to it standing next to Pete! It once happened when Pete's wife Emily was there as well. We all just stood there while Harvey was playing it on full volume. The thing is, he makes you listen to the whole song from start to finish. And if you interrupt him or cut it short, he kicks off. Kids do love to make situations awkward, don't they? But I think we can all see the funny side to it.

There's also an old clip of Pete and Harvey from our reality show where Harvey says, 'Fuck off!' to Pete. Basically, Pete had been taking acting lessons at the time and was practising a line – and that was Harvey's response.

It seems he's always had a potty mouth. He must get it from his mother! I swear a lot. But I obviously don't agree with young children swearing, so I always make an effort not to swear in front of the kids. I have no idea where he got it from, but Harvey can hear something once and he really picks up on it. And then he has a habit of repeating things in the correct context.

So sometimes when he sees Pete he'll find that video on YouTube and play it to everyone. It's really weird, but I think it must be his way of communicating with him. I have no idea how that must make Pete feel. It's strange because if I'm there picking the kids up and Pete comes out, Harvey will relate back to memories that he's had.

He sings nursery rhymes that Pete used to sing with him when he was younger. His memory is amazing. He remembers the smallest details. If he meets a new person, he'll remember their name forever. He never fails to amaze me. Even if it is embarrassing sometimes!

Dwight doesn't play a part in his life which, as you know, he made clear from the very beginning. But I guess there's always been a part of me that's had a glimmer of hope that one day he would admit he'd made a big mistake. I'd never be able to forget what he's done to us, but I'd try and forgive him – for Harvey's sake. It's never too late to make things right.

I just don't understand any men out there who don't want to be involved in their child's life. Even if it's just a one-night stand, that isn't the kid's fault. I guess everyone's view is different.

But as a mum, I don't get it and I never will. We were all kids once – and we all remember things from our childhood and how things can affect you when you're older. I like to be honest with my children about everything and then nothing can ever fall back on you.

Obviously me and Dwight are in the same kind of industry, and it really pisses me off when I bump into people who tell me that he's a nice guy who's doing all these amazing charity events. That may be right but surely it's also important to do something for his own son who has disabilities! It's actually laughable. It's like he's always trying to portray a good image. If I'm honest, I don't know how he sleeps at night. If I knew I had a child out there who I didn't have anything to do with, it would constantly be on my mind.

I've also heard from people that he's told them I've stopped him from seeing Harvey, which could not be further from the truth. That's just a weak excuse and he knows it is.

I actually recently spoke to Andy Cole's wife – Andy is Dwight's good friend and his former teammate. I bumped into her at an event and she told me that Dwight blames me for not letting him see Harvey. But I can honestly say it's never been me. Why the hell wouldn't I want my son to see his dad? I think he just believes his own lies to make himself feel better.

When I did *Celebrity SAS: Who Dares Wins* in 2020, I was on the show with former footballer John Fashanu, who sometimes plays golf with Dwight. I was talking about Harvey to him and he was shocked when I told him that Dwight doesn't see him. So Dwight obviously doesn't tell people the full story. I always think that people who are around Dwight surely must say things to him about Harvey and tell him to get in touch. It's so weird. I can't get my head around it.

Dwight actually spoke to Harvey over the phone on

his tenth birthday. My mum had organised it with his manager. To be honest, I was shocked that it happened. But I think Dwight was even more shocked when Harvey asked him, 'When am I seeing you?' The last time I saw Dwight was in 2012, when I met up with him at a restaurant in Alderley Edge, Cheshire, to speak about Harvey and what Harvey had said on the phone.

I can remember the day very clearly. I arrived at the restaurant and Dwight was already there. I could see him sitting waiting for me at the table. I felt anxious and I didn't really want to be there, but I was doing it for our son. I walked over to him and he didn't really say much – it was so awkward. He hadn't even bought me a drink! But that was typical Dwight. I didn't expect anything less.

We didn't end up having food, it was just a very quick, unfriendly meeting. He was being really arrogant and wouldn't even look at me. I was thinking, 'Why the fuck am I actually even here?' I was talking about Harvey and how he'd made so much progress. I was trying to show Dwight videos of him playing the piano, but he kept saying he didn't want to know. I have no idea why he even agreed to meet me if that was going to be his attitude.

I brought up what Harvey had said to him on his birthday and asked if he would like to start seeing him regularly. And that's when he put the final nail in the coffin and said, 'To be honest, I've disowned you and I've disowned Harvey out of my life. I don't want anything to do with either of you.' Wow. How low can you get?

Even after he said that, I was still trying to be persistent. I wanted Harvey to have his dad in his life, but he just wasn't interested in any of it. 'This isn't about me. This is your son and your flesh and blood,' I said. But he just didn't give a shit. There's only so much you can try before you realise you're flogging a dead horse. I got up and left and that's the last time I saw him. I haven't heard from him since.

But I've never given up. Since then, I've sent him messages on Instagram asking him to come and see Harvey. I've even sent him videos of Harvey speaking to him. How can you live with yourself after ignoring an innocent child like that? I've never heard from his family either. They've never sent a birthday card or anything like that. I always thought he was quite family-oriented, but obviously not. We'd always got on with his family, so it's a shame. It's Harvey I feel for. I'm the only family he has, along with his siblings and of course my side of the family.

There's been many times where I've thought, 'Should I just turn up at Dwight's doorstep with Harvey?' Sometimes I think, 'What the hell have I got to lose?' But I just know it would be a waste of time and a waste of petrol. Alderley Edge is a long way to travel just to be rejected. And to be honest, I don't even know where he lives. He's probably moved since I last saw him. But I must admit, it is very tempting. Then again, why should I be the one to make the effort? I've tried hard enough during all these years. Why should I give him that satisfaction? He knows where we are. But to be honest, he doesn't deserve Harvey. Harvey is incredibly special and anyone would be lucky to have him. I count my blessings every day that he's mine. Dwight has never been a part of his life and he gets zero credit for him. He's done absolutely nothing for him and he should be ashamed.

Dwight has never said anything supportive to me and not once has he told me that I've done a good job. I'm just used to the fact that he was just a sperm donor. He's no father to Harvey.

Along with my other children, Harvey is the best thing that's ever happened to me. It's just a shame Dwight doesn't feel the same way. I've even tried to reach out to his ex, Naomi Smith, who has a 14-year-old son with Dwight called Brandon Tiger, who I believe Dwight sees on a regular basis. I'd really like Harvey to meet his half-brother.

Ironically, Junior and Princess have actually met him. They were in Cyprus on holiday with their dad years ago and they ended up bumping into Naomi. How random is that? She went over to the table to introduce herself and apparently Junior cried his eyes out because he said he couldn't get over the fact he looked so much like Harvey, but obviously smaller. And that's all I know about that. I'd love Naomi to reply to me and for us all to meet up. It's cruel to keep brothers apart.

As much as I'd like Dwight to turn around after all these years and say he wants to make it right, I don't think he ever will. I think if he wanted to build a relationship with Harvey, he would have done it years ago. Also, it would take time for Harvey to be able to get to know him. It wouldn't be like, 'Harvey, here's your dad', and everything's fine. It would have to be a gradual process and Harvey would have to be accompanied by an expert.

He isn't even properly aware of who Dwight is. If I say to him, 'Harvey, who's Dwight?' He'll just respond with, 'I don't know.' He has no emotional connection to him – all he knows of Dwight is the odd photos I've shown him. But I've always said the door is open. My mum asks Dwight's manager if he wants to come and see Harvey on his birthday every year, but it's always the same answer. 'No, he's just not interested.' All I can say is that Dwight has missed out on many years of love and laughter. I pity him.

At least Harvey will always have me. I know this is brutal, but I hope that I outlive Harvey. It's a thought that runs through my mind often. The reason I say it is because I know he wouldn't cope without me. I'm the only one who knows him inside out. I know the way to speak to him, I know the way to cuddle him, I know the way to tickle him. I don't think anyone else could care for him like I do. He wouldn't understand why I wasn't there. And I can't stand the thought of not knowing what would happen to him.

Of course I don't want him to die and it would absolutely kill me, but I think other mums in a similar situation to me will understand what I'm trying to say. At least I understand the concept of death, Harvey doesn't have a clue. He would just cry and cry, and he wouldn't understand where I'd gone.

Before I went into The Priory, I was in a very dark place. I felt suicidal and the only thing that stopped me from going through with it was a picture of my children's faces. If I didn't have children, I wouldn't be here today. They saved me. Harvey saved me. When I was so low, I thought that my other four children would be able to cope without me. Now that I'm in a good place, I know that's irrational thinking. But I knew that Harvey definitely wouldn't be able to cope without me.

He'd be heartbroken without me. Harvey has his brothers and sisters, who would of course look after him, but you can't beat the bond you have with your mum.

Nine

SIBLING BOND

My five beautiful children are my absolute world. Everything I do is for them. I love having a big family. I love the excitement of it and I love how all the kids are so close. There's never a dull moment with us – it really is a madhouse.

As I said before, I always knew I wanted a lot of children. As soon as I had Harvey, I knew that being a mum was my true calling in life. I've always got my hands full, but I wouldn't change it for the world. And trust me, if I can deal with Harvey, I can deal with any child!

After going through such a tough time with Harvey, some might wonder whether it put me off having more kids. But it certainly didn't. If anything, it made me feel like I had even more love and protection to give. When I had Junior, I did worry about how having another baby in the family would affect Harvey's behaviour. It was definitely a shock to his system. I think he found it hard to deal with the fact there was suddenly a baby in the house, making lots of noise and stealing his toys.

When he was younger, Harvey would often hit his siblings. I could never leave him alone with them just in case he did lash out. Because of his strength and size, I was worried he could really hurt them, though of course he would never mean to. Just like any other siblings, they'd argue and fight, but they got on well most of the time and would play together nicely.

I did also worry that the children would miss out on my attention because Harvey needed so much care. But they've always been very good at understanding that he does need to be treated differently. I never wanted to leave Harvey out, but inevitably, if we ever went anywhere, the whole day became about making sure he was okay. And it's still like that now. That's why it would have been nice if Dwight was in his life, so he could have taken some of the pressure off.

As anyone who has a disabled child will know, it's important to have a break from caring for them sometimes. It can be very full-on. I don't think carers get enough credit. It's not that I ever wanted to get rid of

Harvey, but because I sometimes felt that the other kids suffered.

Now that he's older, it is slightly easier as the other kids know exactly what Harvey is like and they're really good with him. Even from a young age, Junior was brilliant at sharing his toys with Harvey and Princess was good at showing him affection. She used to always give him kisses, which he loved.

Harvey is very close to his brothers and sisters. He misses them a lot when they're with their dads. He loves being around them all and even though he loves his own space sometimes, he can become quite bored when they're out. Each of them knows how to deal with Harvey and we all know his quirky little sayings. The way we communicate with him would be alien to anyone else. Other people must be like, 'What the hell are they on about?!' For example, we always have to finish off his sentences.

'Oh my…' Harvey says, and we have to say, 'God.' Or he'll say, 'Hip hip…' and we say, 'Hurray.'

Another funny example of this is that Harvey always brings up the Queen's Diamond Jubilee from years ago. He remembers watching a concert on the TV and he remembers exactly who performed and in what order.

He mentions the fact that Gary Barlow performed. So if he says 'Gary', he expects us all to reply with 'Barlow'.

And if we don't, he gets mad at us. He's so tuned in to everything. Harvey lives in his own world, and if you don't know his world and don't say what he wants you to say, then God help you.

He knows when I'm taking the piss with him as well. Sometimes I like to wind him up and have a bit of fun with him. He says, 'Mum, don't. Mummy's only joking, isn't she?' So I say, 'Okay, yes Harvey. I'm only joking.'

All of my children have completely different personalities. I love that they're unique in their own ways – especially Harvey. I don't even know how to describe him. Harvey is just Harvey! He's loved by so many people.

It's funny because even though he's the big brother, he listens to all his siblings – even the younger ones, Jett and Bunny. Bunny definitely likes to tell him off and point her finger! He's so gentle with Bunny, though. He always calls her 'Bunny Bops', which is so sweet. Harvey loves watching cartoons, especially *Peppa Pig,* so that's something he often does with Jett and Bunny.

It chops and changes all the time, but currently, out of all of Harvey's siblings, Princess probably spends the most time with him. She's so good with him as she talks to him and calms him down like I do. She's really relaxed with him.

I can bang on as much as I like about Harvey and his siblings, but I thought it would be really nice for Princess to have her say and give her own thoughts on what it's like to have a brother with complex needs. So, over to you, Princess...

'We absolutely love our big brother, Harvey. We have so much fun together, but it can be difficult at times with his disabilities. He can be quite hard to look after. If people don't know him, they don't know how to calm him down when he kicks off.

If we all go out together as a family, it can be really hard work for Mum. But we all know how to talk to him – even Jett and Bunny do. It's because we've grown up with him and we don't know any different. We just know the tone of voice to use with him and we know exactly what to say. If he kicks off, I'll say something like, 'Harv, if you carry on then you won't get your iPad.' We don't bribe him, but the way to deal with him is that he has to understand there's going to be a consequence.

Or I say, 'If you're good you can have a treat.' He absolutely loves carrot cake. As I've gotten older, I've learnt how to communicate with him and calm him down. But I do try and let Mum sort him out when he's kicking off, because she knows him better than anyone.

Harvey is also really close to Junior. He's good at talking to Harvey and he listens to him. Harvey is the oldest, but Junior is sort of like his older brother. Sometimes Harvey will start making noises and you can see in his eyes when he's not in a good mood. Bunny will say to him, 'Harv, stop it.' And then he says, 'OK, Bunny.' He does listen to her. But obviously she's a lot younger, so she doesn't really know how to control him.

Once he gets into a temper, Bunny and Jett try to avoid him because sometimes it can be hard to know how he's going to react. He's much bigger than them, so they find it scary. We know that he can't help it and it's not that they don't want to be with him, but they like to stay away if he's in a bad mood.

Harvey loves the sound of crying, so sometimes he can purposely go for Jett and Bunny just to make them cry. Obviously he can't help it and he's not doing it to purposely hurt them, he just enjoys the noise of it.

He used to do that to me when I was younger, too. I can't really remember what it was like when I was really young, but when I was about seven, he used to try and hit me. It's because he used to hear me and Junior play fighting together when we were younger, so he worked out that if he hit me it would make me cry. He can be really clever.

He's also absolutely hilarious – and you can actually have a really funny conversation with him. He makes me laugh so much. He's definitely got banter. But then his mood can switch really quickly. One minute he can be happy, and then the next he can be kicking off because something small has happened. For example, if a song comes on that he doesn't like. It can be quite scary for us because he starts smashing things up.

Harvey likes being active, so he enjoys coming out with us and doing activities. But only if it's something he wants to do. If we ask him if he wants to go for a walk, it just depends on how he feels on the day. If he says no, then you can't really argue with it because there's not much persuading him.

He definitely knows what he does and doesn't want. If it's to do with trains, he'll be very excited, but if it's something he's not interested in, he'll just kick off if he's made to do it. He absolutely loves trains. We once went on the Gatwick Express together and he loved it. It's interesting though, because he hates the noise of doors banging, but if a door bangs on a train he doesn't acknowledge it and he doesn't really mind.

He also loves frogs – he's always drawing them on his iPad. He's such a good drawer. Because he's partially blind, I don't know how he does it. He's obsessed with his iPad. I think it's literally his everything. If he doesn't have his iPad, then he's not in a good mood.

Unfortunately, Harvey gets loads of hate online, which is horrible. People don't say it to our faces, but they say stuff behind a computer screen. They wouldn't dare say it to Harvey's face. They're cowards. He's actually so innocent and people don't realise that. I don't get why people feel the need to be so nasty towards him. Some of my friends have taken the mickey out of him in the past, but they're not really my friends if they do that. But Harvey also gets a lot of love online, too, which is really nice to see. He deserves it.

Harvey is very loving and he's always asking for cuddles. He says, 'Princess, I need you,' and I'm like, 'Why do you need me, Harv?' And he says, 'Cuddles. I love cuddles.' He's very affectionate towards my mum. He loves her cuddles and kisses. He gets upset when he's not with her, but she FaceTimes him every day and he knows that he can just call her when he wants.

I've always been close with Harvey and spent time with him, but over the past couple of years we've become really close. I know he's my older brother, but I feel really protective of him. I love him to bits and I wouldn't change him for the world.

He's gone off to college now and I do worry about him being in a new environment, but I know it's an exciting time for him. I'll miss him, but I'll still go and visit him.

We all love you so much, Harv. And I'm so proud to call you my brother.'

Ten

HARVEY'S LAW

'Apparently Jordan and Peter Andre are fighting over custody of Harvey. Eventually one of them will lose and have to keep him. I have a theory Jordan married a cage fighter because she needed someone strong enough to stop Harvey from fucking her.'

I can hardly bring myself to repeat those words, but that was the 'joke' the so-called comedian Frankie Boyle told on his Channel 4 show in 2010. I would never choose to take the time out of my day to listen to his material, but it was brought to my attention.

When I first heard it, I just thought, 'Wow. How could someone do that? How could anyone be so vulgar about an innocent child?' It was disgusting. There was a public outcry and it received more than 500 complaints to the broadcaster.

This is the same man who said about me, 'Ah Katie Price. A bit of a Marmite figure. Half the country hates her, and the other half thinks she belongs on the end of a knife.' You can make 'jokes' about me all you like. I can take it, but don't you dare make a joke about my son.

I wanted people to see just how much it affected our family, so I filmed a documentary about the whole thing called *Standing Up For Harvey*. I had a brilliant response from viewers. I think a lot of people saw me for the first time as a mum, rather than the celebrity they'd read about in the media.

During filming, I interviewed other comedians and spoke to mums who had children with disabilities to hear their stories. I also met with representatives from charities, including Mencap, who Harvey is now an ambassador for. I met up with a group of young people with disabilities at a support group run by the charity. They told me how they'd been very cruelly bullied and called names. And that's exactly what Frankie did to my son.

I invited him to meet us so that he could see what we go through on a daily basis with Harvey. I wanted him to understand how we deal with his complex needs and why, as a family, we were so upset that he had made him the butt of his joke. But surprise surprise, I heard nothing from him. Despite asking several times, I never received an apology from Frankie and I still haven't to this day. I think it's fair to say I've given up waiting for that one.

Ofcom acknowledged that it appeared to mock Harvey, but that's as far as it went. They didn't force Channel 4 to apologise – which was just plain insulting. Apparently Channel 4's chief executive even admitted that he had personally signed off the joke.

Channel 4 had Frankie on their show, making disgusting statements like that, yet in their ad breaks they were promoting the Paralympics. It's like, how can you promote an event like that and then have a comedian mocking disability at the same time? It just doesn't make sense and it comes across as totally insincere.

As a dad himself, Frankie should know better. A family member of his could get run over and be paralysed, and then he'd become their carer for the rest of their lives. I wonder if he'd mock a disability then? If he's going to make fun of someone, at least make fun of someone who's got a right to reply. That's my argument with Harvey. He gets mocked and trolled, but he can't defend himself and it's cruel. I'm all about having a laugh and a bit of banter – I can take a joke. But you know when you're stepping over the line.

I've been in the industry for over 20 years, so I'm used

to people saying bad things about me. I'd get horrible stuff written about me in the press and people would send me hate mail. And then social media came along and suddenly anyone could say anything about anyone.

Over the last few years especially, social media has blown up and has given vile trolls a platform to bully people. The trolling Harvey receives online is horrendous. People started mocking him in every single way and I just didn't understand how they were able to get away with it. I've done so much investigation into trolling in the past, and there are so many people who take their own lives because of it. Even children.

I get trolled all the time and trust me, I've had it bad. But I'm used to it and I can handle it. I've become immune to it, which is also bad. No one should become immune to abuse. When it comes to my children, I'll do anything I can to protect them from it. Especially Harvey, who can't protect himself. Funnily enough, it seems to be grown men who attack him. It's usually football fans as well. How pathetic is that?

I feel sorry for the trolls. I genuinely believe they have some kind of mental illness. I would love to meet a troll, sit them down, and ask them what goes through their head. But I don't think any of them would have the balls to say anything to my face. It's so wrong.

I think a lot of people set up fake accounts just to try

and get a rise out of me. I'm not silly, I can tell when people are just trying to wind me up. But I like to name and shame the trolls. I usually share the accounts that actually look legitimate, and the ones who have said something about Harvey more than once. I have a lot more power than people think because when I share their details, it reaches a lot of people.

I set Harvey up with his own Instagram account when he turned 16, as he'd been asking me for one for ages. Every time he did a drawing, he'd ask, 'Can Mummy put that on Instagram?' I was hesitant about making him an account for a while. But when he reached that age, I just thought, 'Actually, why shouldn't he be able to have an account like other teenagers?'

Some people question why I would let him have a public account and allow him to be subject to abuse when I'm campaigning against it, but why should he be hidden away? My argument has always been that he shouldn't be isolated just because he's got disabilities. He shouldn't be treated any differently.

Thankfully, Harvey doesn't understand online abuse, but I block accounts and delete any vile comments on his page. I like to show off his wonderful personality as he really is one of a kind. He's recently learnt how to 'flip the bird', AKA, give someone the middle finger. But Harvey thinks it's your index finger, so now he keeps putting up

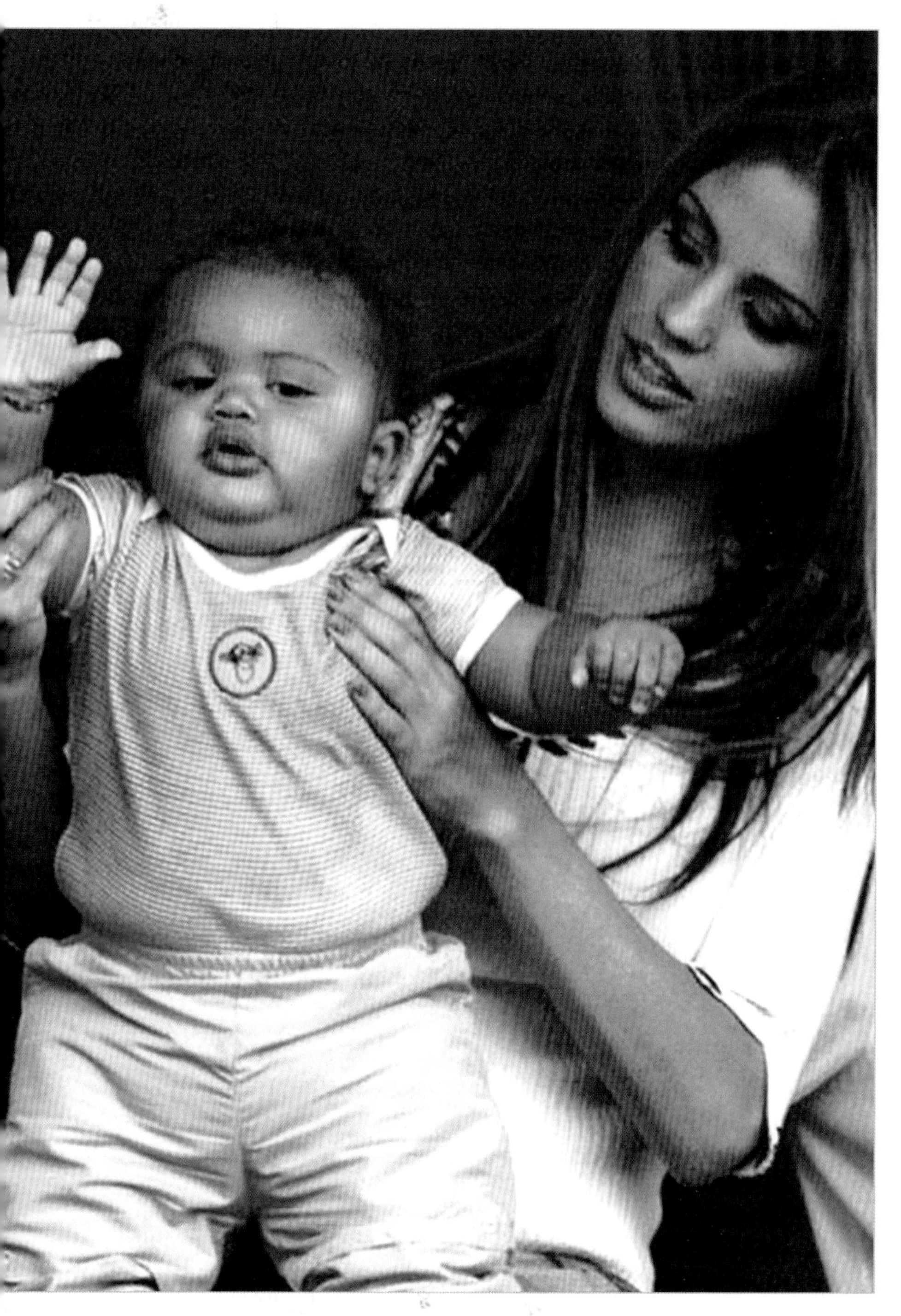

rvey was such a gorgeous baby! This was his first of many high fives

Top left: Me and Harvey playing 'pat a cake, pat a cake, baker's man'. He still loves this song. **Top right:** My beautiful little boy. He was such a goo baby

Bottom: Harvey's first trip to a Soccer Six tournament. I remember he loved all the attention he was getting from fans and friends

ɔsolutely love this picture of me and Harvey, he looks so happy and sweet

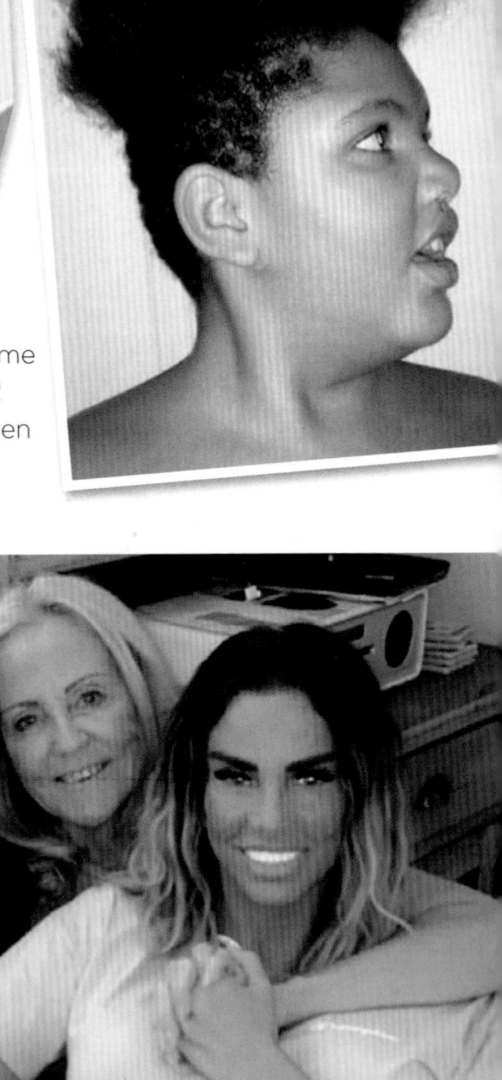

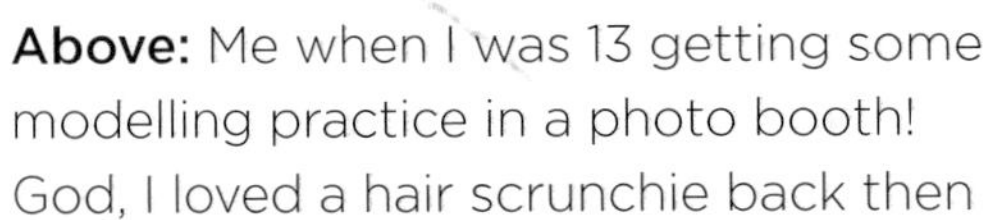

Above: Me when I was 13 getting some modelling practice in a photo booth! God, I loved a hair scrunchie back then

Right: My ultra-cool dude! Harvey rocked this hairstyle

Above: Me and my sister, Sophie, celebrating our mum's birthday with the best cake! My mum loves yoga, so this cake was perfect for her

Top: Love my two girls, Princess and Bunny! They are so like me, they love getting dressed up and having their hair and make-up done

Left: My handsome and talented son, Junior! I admire his confidence so much and have loved seeing him grow into a young man

Left: Harvey has always ha an obsession with trains, particularly the Gatwick Express. His drawings of trains are amazing. Wel done, Harvey

Above: This picture is a family favourite from Harvey – Dad's work truck! Grandad was very proud of him

Left: Harvey always draws the best frog pictures

Harvey enjoyed supporting the NHS throughout lockdown in 2020

ight: Harvey getting ready for hristmas with his drawing of Santa

elow: Did I mention that Harvey also ves to draw cars? I love the little haracters he creates who drive them

Left: I can't believe I made it into the semi-finals of MasterChef. I'm so proud of myself, what an achievemer Thank you to my sister's boyfriend, Harry, for teachir me how to cook via Zoom during lockdown before the show! Your teaching paid o

Top: Harvey's favourite treat. Who doesn't love a Mr Whippy ice cream?

Above: Pasta has always been one of Harvey's favourite dinners, especially with loads of cheese on top!

bove: Harvey loves a selfie with Mummy bear

Left: Harvey at his 18th birthday party with a giant frog!

Above: Harvey opening some of his presents with me

Above: Harvey blowing out the candles of his 18th birthday cake – he loves rainbows, too

Right: The most perfect cake for my Harvey Price

bove: Love this pic with the kids! **Bottom:** Happy birthday, Harvey

Top: My gorgeous children

Above: Bunny and Harvey have such an amazing bond, I love seeing them play together

Right: Kisses for Bunny from her big brother

Above: Hot tub fun for the kids

Left: I adore my mum, we have such a special bond

Bottom: Cuddles with Harvey

Harvey's first ever National Television Awards red carpet moment

Above: Happy times with my baby bear, Harvey

Left: Stamp out online trolling! Something Harvey and I feel very passionate about #HarveysLaw

Bottom: Me and Harvey hitting the red carpet

bove: Kisses for Harvey Price

Harvey and Me
– everyone's
favourite picture

his second finger. It's so funny because obviously it's not the real thing, and he doesn't really understand it.

But I love to show that side of him online. A lot of the things he says have been turned into 'memes' now, or whatever the kids call them. Some are just a bit of fun and we can all laugh because we know that it's not mocking him, but others take it too far and it's just obvious they're taking the piss out of him.

In 2016, I appeared on *Loose Women* with Harvey to talk about online bullying. I'm always so nervous about doing live television with Harvey, because you just never know what he's going to say.

Backstage, I said to him, 'Harvey, no swearing today please.'

'Yes, Mummy,' he replied.

But on air, as most of you will have probably seen, it was a whole different story. I asked him, 'Harvey, if someone says something horrible to you. What do you say?' and his response was, 'Hello, you c***.' I was mortified! Some might argue that his reply was pretty accurate. I got loads of messages afterwards from people saying, 'Good boy, Harvey. That's exactly what they are,' and, 'Well done, Harvey.' But I felt so bad that he had dropped the C-bomb on live television.

I think if we were to go on again now that he's older, he'd listen to me if I told him not to swear. I don't think he understood it properly back then. Well, I say he wouldn't swear, but I couldn't promise that! Who would have thought that five years later it's become Harvey's most memorable line?! I can definitely laugh about it now, but I'm laughing with him and not at him. That's the difference.

I was surprised, and saddened, to see that the cricketer Ben Stokes had made fun of Harvey because of it. He publicly mocked him in a Snapchat video in 2017. He was filmed doing an impression of Harvey saying, 'Hello, you c***' and it circulated online.

What Frankie Boyle did was horrendous, but he was known for making vile, unfunny jokes. I didn't know Ben, I'd never met him and I couldn't understand why he would do something like that. He's recently gone through his own mental health struggles, which is sad, but he caused us a lot of hurt with what he did.

After it all came out, he wrote to me to say sorry and offered to meet us to apologise, which is better than what Frankie did. But I said no. To be honest, I thought he was only sorry because he got caught. He shouldn't have done it in the first place. He then made a public apology, probably to make himself feel better. What he did was disgusting and a real low blow. Again, he's a dad himself and he should know better.

There have been so many horrible things that have

been said and posted about Harvey – there are too many to write down, and some of them I wouldn't even want to repeat.

One that sticks out in my memory is when a troll altered a picture of a bag of Haribo Tangfastics to read, 'Harveybo Tangspastics.' They then wrote alongside it, 'I've got some sweets for Harvey here. I hope he chokes on them.'

It was shocking. Why would anyone say that? He's also been made into derogatory memes about sex. Who the hell uses a young, disabled person's picture to make a joke about sex? It's below the belt.

Another troll Photoshopped Harvey's head onto the body of a Freddo chocolate bar, while someone else mocked-up a picture of him on a *King Kong* DVD and changed it to 'King Mong'.

Someone has to sit down and take the time out of their day to make these pictures and videos. I just don't understand what goes through their heads. It's evil. He gets a lot of racist abuse, too.

'What's black and screams?'

'Harvey Price answering the iron.'

That was a 'joke' that went around online and got shared thousands of times. He's also constantly being called the N-word. It's just absolutely horrific.

When I went on *This Morning* about four years ago

to talk about the abuse Harvey receives, I asked Phillip Schofield how he would feel if someone called his child a 'spastic n****r.' He was shocked at what I'd said. I repeated it again and he told me to stop saying it.

Why? Because it was a horrible thing to hear. But the only reason it was so shocking is because I was saying it out loud. Why isn't there that same reaction when it's written down? I'm asked to stop saying it on TV, yet people can write it on social media, send it to me, and nothing gets done about it.

It got to the point where I just couldn't keep seeing all this abuse and sit back. I kept calling out the trolls on my social media, but something more needed to be done.

I was speaking to my mum about it and we both just said, 'This has got to stop now.' After seeking help from the police, I was shocked to learn that no charges could be pressed against these people – and that's when we started Harvey's Law together.

We set up a petition and we were so happy when it got over 100,000 signatures in just a few days. When I look back at my career and everything I've achieved, Harvey's Law is one of the things I'm most proud of.

In a nutshell, we're fighting so that trolls face consequences for their actions. Online abuse should be a criminal offence. To me, it's a no-brainer. It's not just for Harvey, it's for everyone from all walks of life. But we just wanted to put it in Harvey's name because he's the motivation behind it after all the terrible abuse he receives.

I just think it's so disgusting that people are allowed to get away with trolling without being punished. Of course I believe in freedom of speech, but this is just plain bullying. Convicted paedophiles are on a register – and I think trolls should be prosecuted and go on a register too, because everyone should know what kind of people they are. For example, if you went for a job interview and they really liked you, I'm sure they'd look at you differently if they could see that you've trolled people online. Why would anyone want to employ a bully?

It was amazing to get the backing of MPs for Harvey's Law. The House of Commons Petitions Committee agreed that the laws around the issue of online abuse weren't fit for purpose, and we took it to Parliament. Oh my God, I was so nervous!

When you walk into the House of Commons, it all feels very serious. I like to have a bit of a joke and banter, but that is not the place for banter. You sit there with all these important people and say your piece. I was worried I might stick out like a sore thumb, but my mum and I did a really good job – if I do say so myself!

I never dreamed in a million years I'd be able to do that. Even Harvey doesn't realise that we're fighting to have a law in his name. Like I said, he has no understanding of online trolling and I'm so glad he doesn't. But my worry is that online bullying can easily progress. If someone went up to him in the street and said something nasty like, 'You're fat and you're stupid,' he would understand that and that would really hurt him. Or if someone said, 'Your drawings are horrible,' he would get very upset.

We started Harvey's Law back in 2018, and while I'm proud of what we've achieved so far, we're still fighting for it. I'll be honest, though, the trolling has actually gotten worse over the past few years.

There was a couple from Aberdeen who filmed themselves last year mocking Harvey. The video was horrific. A woman was pretending to be me while her partner was pretending to be Harvey, saying, 'Hello you c***.' I found it absolutely disgusting because not only did he mimic Harvey's eye movements and how he speaks, he also painted his face brown – which is clearly extremely racist. They were arrested, but I was shocked to find out the police dropped the charges on them because they said there wasn't enough evidence. That's mind-blowing to me. Surely video evidence couldn't be any more clear.

A man who shared the video on social media also got arrested and actually ended up going to court. I know he wasn't involved in making the video, but personally, I think sharing it is just as bad.

I went along to the court case in June as I wanted to confront the bully. I stood up in court and I was cross-examined. I was nervous, but I really tried to get my point across. I said to the courtroom, 'For those of you who have kids, you'll understand that as a mother, seeing my son being publicly mocked makes me angry. All I'm trying to do is protect him and help protect everyone else.'

Unfortunately, he was found not guilty. It was so disappointing. He claimed he only shared it as a joke and didn't mean to cause offence. Apparently that's a good enough excuse. The judge should have made an example of him.

It just makes me feel like if people know they can get away with it, then they'll continue to do it. It was a huge slap in the face, and I felt like all the trolls out there were probably thinking, 'Ha! We can get away with it.'

But it only drives me forward. I'm trying my best and I'll continue to stick up for Harvey – and for everyone else. Sadly, not everyone's case even makes it to court. But I would say to anyone out there that if you're being trolled, just make sure you document everything you can so that you can build a case and go to the police with it.

From what I've seen, none of my other children are targeted online. People just take aim at Harvey because he's vulnerable and they're pathetic cowards. Sometimes on a completely unrelated post that doesn't even have anything to do with Harvey, trolls will still write things about him.

A couple of years ago, I was selling my pink Barbie Jeep on eBay. I got a company to sort it out and set it all up for me and it was all good. It got about 200,000 views in two days and it got loads of bids. But we were forced to take it down because the car dealership was bombarded with abuse.

Nope, not about the car. Not about me. About Harvey. It was disgusting and totally uncalled for. People were sending messages like, 'Has Harvey licked the windows?' and, 'I hope it's been cleaned if Harvey has been in there.' How the hell does selling my car have anything to do with Harvey? It makes me feel sick to my stomach.

Worst of all, police officers have even mocked my son. In July, a group of officers were investigated after taking the piss out of Harvey in a WhatsApp group. It's completely disgusting. They deserved to be named and shamed, and sacked. These are the people who are supposed to protect us. If you can't trust the police, who can you trust? I put out a video of Harvey to show everyone how it affects our family. I told him that some police officers had been nasty to Harvey and he said, 'I don't like the police being horrible to Harvey.' It's heartbreaking.

I think the reason people still continue to troll is

because there's still no consequence for it. I think all we need is for one person to be prosecuted, and then it would make people think twice.

Another reason is because people can just hide behind an anonymous account. So that's why earlier this year, I also launched my Track A Troll petition with the help of my mum. It's different to Harvey's Law because with this, we're campaigning to make it compulsory for people to provide ID before being able to set up a social media account.

If you're buying a house or a car, you have to show your identity. They want to know all your details so that if you don't pay your bills, they know where to find you. So why should it be different with social media? If you're going to be making horrible comments online and someone makes a complaint about you – you should be able to be tracked.

Every sane person knows it needs to be in place, but sadly these things take time. And unfortunately, during this time, it will continue and it's only going to get worse. But I'll never give up.

I've had a lot of support from the press when it comes to backing my campaigns, but in the past they've been part of the problem, too. Back in 2007, *Heat Magazine* was giving away free stickers to their readers. It sounds completely harmless, right? Wrong.

The stickers were very offensive. We're talking the same wavelength as Frankie Boyle. For example, one was a picture of Britney Spears with a shaved head and it said alongside the image, 'Mum of the year.'

I was so shocked and upset to see that Harvey was also included in the stickers. They'd cut out a picture of Harvey's face and written next to it, 'Harvey wants to eat me!' I just couldn't believe a magazine like that was making fun of an innocent child with disabilities. They were openly mocking his weight, which is caused by his complex needs.

They received a lot of complaints and I think they realised very quickly they had made a huge error of judgment. How not one person at *Heat* looked at that and thought, 'Hang on a minute. That's not right,' I do not know. The magazine apologised publicly and they made a donation to Vision Charity.

I've had to deal with a lot of shit when it comes to Harvey being mocked, abused and bullied. But on top of that, I've also had to deal with kidnap threats involving Harvey. Online abuse is horrific, but a lot of the time they are just empty threats. These were *very* real threats – and they were terrifying.

I've had three in total. The first time it happened was in 2006. The police told us that their intelligence revealed there was a kidnap threat against us. I honestly thought it was some kind of practical joke at first. But no, it was deadly serious.

They believed four people were involved in the plot and they were planning to do it while I was in the car with Harvey and Junior. The police revealed the gang were planning to force me off the road and seize Harvey and then demand a £1 million ransom. We were told the gang had been watching us and knew all of our movements. They even knew where Harvey's school was. It was utterly terrifying. Scotland Yard had to take Harvey to school every day because he needed to be closely watched. My life had to change dramatically. I had to step up security in the house and I had police protection with me at all times. The feeling of being unsafe in your own home is awful.

The second threat was a very similar thing. I couldn't believe it was happening again. Scotland Yard contacted us to tell us there was a gang who were planning a plot on Harvey. They would stage a car accident and take him. At the time, I was advised to never stop the car while I was driving and if I was in traffic, to make sure I wasn't bumper to bumper with another car. I always had to leave space so that if I needed to, I could swerve and get out. I've been taught the art of kidnap evasion. Even to this day, I would know exactly how to get out of a kidnap situation if I had to.

I talk about it so blasé now, because I'm just used to it. But I do still have that feeling of looking over my shoulder – I don't think that will ever go away. The third threat was specifically about kidnapping me.

That time, it was a gang from Liverpool and the police told me they knew exactly when I would be leaving my house. Apparently they even knew all the building plans of the house so they could work out where each room was. Scotland Yard had to move in with me while it was going on, but as you can imagine I had many sleepless nights.

I've also received blackmail plots about Harvey. I was once sent an anonymous email which threatened to kidnap him if I didn't pay them £50,000. They said they were going to find Harvey and slash his face. The police ended up tracking the email back to an address, but the woman who lived there denied having any knowledge of the threat and nothing came of it.

This is why I feel like I constantly need to have security, and why I have my protection dog, Blade. But the thing is, you can have all the protection in the world, but if something like that is going to happen, then there's not much you can do about it. By the time you've called the police, it could be too late.

I think these criminals target Harvey because they know about his medical needs and how vulnerable he is.

They know exactly what they're doing with these threats. Harvey needs his medication to survive, so it was all very scary. To be honest, he wouldn't be easy to kidnap now because he's so big and he'd kick off. But when he was younger, he wouldn't have understood it.

We live in a very cruel world where not everyone is nice, and it's hard to teach Harvey that. Harvey is so innocent and gentle, it breaks my heart that anyone would want to hurt him. But I will continue to fight for him and protect him for the rest of my life.

Eleven

EDUCATING HARVEY

Despite Harvey's disabilities, I've always wanted him to have the best education possible so that he can reach his full potential.

I did everything I could to try and help him progress. I always knew that a mainstream school would never be an option, so it's been very hard finding somewhere that can cater to his complex needs.

Harvey's education started at Dorton House in Sevenoaks. This was a special school for blind or visually impaired children that was run by the charity Royal London Society For Blind People.

Me and my mum started taking him there for drop-in

sessions when he was about two years old. We'd go there and meet other families with blind or visually impaired children. We'd all sit around in a circle and do activities with our toddlers, like singing songs and playing instruments. It was a really good chance to talk to other mums who were going through a similar experience, because I didn't know anyone around me who had a disabled child.

When I ran the London Marathon in 2009, I used the money I raised to buy a minibus for Dorton House. We also built a park there so that there was a play area for the children. Every time I raise money for charity, I always prefer to ask them what they need rather than just giving them the money. That way, I know it doesn't just get swallowed up in admin and it's actually worthwhile.

I also only work with charities that I can associate with. I get asked to do lots of charity work, and while I hate turning it down, I'd rather concentrate on the ones that I'm already involved in. I feel really bad saying no, but I've realised you can't say yes to everything, because someone's going to get upset at one point. I end up having to let people down, and that's not fair.

The London Marathon is one of the hardest things I've ever done. I did it again in 2018, this time for the British Lung Foundation after my mum was diagnosed with idiopathic pulmonary fibrosis. I dressed in a giant lung costume, but I didn't end up finishing it because of a knee injury. I got a lot of stick, with people accusing me of not bothering to train for it. But that wasn't the case. I tried my best. I raised awareness and my mum was proud of me, so that's the main thing. It's tough, but I'd definitely do it again. The atmosphere is incredible. There's so many people running for so many different charities and the crowds are amazing.

Anyway, when Harvey got a little bit older, he began nursery full-time at Dorton House and stayed at the school right up until it closed down in 2013. He absolutely loved it there and the staff were brilliant. Although we did have to fight the council to get them to pay for Harvey's fees, which has become a frequent thing throughout Harvey's education.

It was a really sad time when it shut because he'd been going there since he was a baby and it became a huge part of his life. But in the last couple of years, we could tell it was heading into a closure. Sadly, a lot of the teachers had been made redundant and they just couldn't afford to keep it going. I don't have one bad word to say about Dorton House. They really helped Harvey and were a vital part of his development.

It was a stressful time for us because I was worried about how Harvey would cope with the sudden change. He shows real progress when he has a regular structure and I didn't want it to set him back. Plus, we didn't have a place elsewhere for him and I knew it would be a nightmare trying to find somewhere that would accommodate his needs. And it was.

We visited a couple of schools nearby but they just didn't feel right. I just couldn't see Harvey being there. Dorton House had definitely set a high standard. When we initially found out the school was closing, some of the parents got together and we discussed the idea of trying to save the school, but unfortunately we couldn't make it work.

We also looked at the possibility of setting up a Free School for children with special needs. We started raising money, but the Government turned it down on the grounds that we didn't have enough pupils to make it worthwhile, which I personally didn't agree with.

After a lot of searching, I finally found a school in Wimbledon called Linden Lodge, which we loved instantly. It had everything we were looking for. The classrooms were bright and cheery, which the other schools we had visited lacked.

They also had a library which catered specifically to blind children, as well as a sensory garden. However, it wasn't as simple as just sending off an application. When you have a disabled child, you feel like you have to fight for everything for them. Because we weren't from the area, we had to go to a tribunal and prove that no other school near us could accommodate Harvey – which we did.

When we were doing Harvey's statement for the school with the local authority and his doctors, they worked out that it would cost around £430,000 a year for Harvey to go to the school. In comparison, the average funding for a disabled child is around £60,000 a year. So that just goes to show how complex Harvey is. It doesn't really get more expensive than that. It's because of all the medication he's on and because of how unpredictable his behaviour is. He needs 24-hour care, which isn't cheap.

They actually told me I should be proud of myself for doing it on my own for all these years without any help. People often ask me, 'How do you do it?' But it's just because he's my son and I don't know any different. I've just made it work. Don't get me wrong, it's been really, really hard, but I've done it. I don't ever want sympathy, I just get on with it.

I was worried about the transition for Harvey, but it wasn't the first time he had experienced going to a new school. In 2009, we went to Los Angeles for three months as I was filming our reality show *Katie & Peter: Stateside*, so I had to find somewhere temporary for him.

I could have just got him a private tutor instead, but I wanted him to socialise with other children. My mum helped me research American schools which would be suitable for Harvey and we found one called the Junior Blind Of America school. It was perfect and he had a brilliant time there. We've been back in Los Angeles since and Harvey still remembers the school. He even remembers his classroom and the names of the teachers. It's quite impressive.

Harvey did kick off in the mornings a few times in his first couple of weeks at Linden Lodge, which was expected. But as soon as he got to school, he absolutely loved it.

The staff there were amazing. He had a teacher who worked with him on a one-to-one basis. She was so good with him and Harvey absolutely loved her. But it wasn't smooth sailing. On her first day with Harvey, he massively kicked off. She actually turned around and said, 'I can't work with him. I'd rather be sent home.' People might think I'm exaggerating when I say Harvey is hard work, but that's how difficult he can be.

Thank God she persisted with him. They really clicked and she was with him for six years. In fact, she often helped me out on weekends and during holidays as well if I needed someone to stay with Harvey due to work commitments.

She became like a family member, as she's been on holidays with us. It's just so that I have an extra pair of hands so I can do things with the other children. If Harvey is in a bad mood, he just refuses to leave the hotel room and we can't force him to do something he doesn't want to do. If he wakes up and he doesn't want to do something, there's no persuading him. He puts on a sad voice and says, 'No, thank you.' And that's not fair on everyone else. We can't just sit inside all day when we're on holiday.

Linden Lodge was perfect, the only downside was that it was so far away. It's funny saying that now, because compared to his new college, it was just around the corner!

It was an hour's drive away and he used to have to travel there and back every day. He had his own driver and my mum used to go on the commute with him. She travelled with him for the first year or so, which I can't thank her for enough. I couldn't be the one to get him ready and take him to school because he would want to spend the whole day with me and just refuse to go to school.

The driver was funded by the Government, which caused a public row when I was in the *Celebrity Big Brother* house in 2015. I was discussing Harvey and how he had a driver who took him to and from the school. Katie Hopkins butted in, asking me if I provided it privately. I explained it would be very expensive to do that and it would cost me up to £1,000 a day.

She turned around and said, 'With the amount you

earn, I'd find that tricky as you could afford it yourself.' To be honest, I didn't expect anything less from her. Two years earlier she had ignorantly said, 'Behind every fat child is a fat mother.' I criticised her at the time, not knowing I'd be locked up in a house with her a couple of years later.

I actually think I did a pretty good job at biting my lip and staying cool with Katie, but I was raging inside. As I said to her, I pay my taxes, and I pay a lot in tax, so why shouldn't I? It's an entitlement that is given to every disabled child in the country, so why should Harvey be different just because I am his mum?

Little did I know, there was a huge debate going on in the outside world. Some people agreed with Katie, but I received so many messages of support, especially from parents with special needs children. Anyone should walk a day in our shoes before judging us. I don't think Katie would last a day. And for the record, I've never claimed any disability living allowance for Harvey – which I have every right to.

But back to Harvey's school. The journey there became increasingly difficult. It got to the point where Harvey started kicking off pretty much every single day.

If he didn't want to go to school, he'd break something or smash the car up. He worked out that if he caused a scene, he wouldn't have to go to school and he'd get a day off. He definitely knew how to manipulate a situation. I'd wake up and I just didn't know what mood he'd be in. It would affect the other kids too because they became scared of him. He was big and he was throwing things around and it wasn't fair on anyone.

There was one day in particular where he was uncontrollably kicking off and I just couldn't calm him down. I ended up having to cancel all my work that day because I had to stay home with him. When it got really bad, he would miss school for about two weeks at a time, so I was worried about it having a negative impact on his learning.

I've looked after Harvey all his life, but I've had crisis points where it's all become too much for me to handle on my own.

When you have disabilities, you have a social assessment team around you. There have been times I've had to call them and tell them I'm finding it hard to cope. This day was one of those times. I phoned the doctors at Maudsley Hospital and Great Ormond Street and explained how Harvey was refusing to get in the car and go to school.

I ended up saying, 'Enough is enough. I can't do this. It's a danger for him and a danger for everyone around him.' They advised me that it could be an option to consider putting Harvey into residential care at the school

Monday to Friday, which would mean he wouldn't have to travel because he would already be there.

I'd always said that Harvey would stay at home with me for the rest of his life. I was totally against the idea. It took me a long time to be convinced that actually, it could be a good thing. If it was up to me, I wouldn't have done it. I guess I was a bit selfish in a way and just wanted him with me. But I had to do what was best for Harvey and in 2019, he started going to residential.

I couldn't do it at home any more for seven days a week. But I just want to make it very clear that I didn't put him into a care home. I never have and I never will. A lot of people mistake it for that.

The school had a boarding section called Richley House, so he stayed there from Monday to Friday and came home every weekend and during the holidays. The biggest issue for us was getting him in the car to travel to school, so it resolved that. If he woke up in a bad mood, it didn't matter as much because he was already on site.

Once he started staying at Richley House, he'd still kick off in the mornings, but he settled in well. He always enjoyed school when he was there, it was just the anxiety of going. Mondays were his least favourite days because he'd just finished a weekend at home with me and it took him a bit of time to get into the routine again. I'm sure many people feel that way about Mondays!

I missed him so much and it was a big change for the family, but I knew it was the best place for him to be. I would FaceTime him every morning and every evening, which I still do now, and he'd constantly send pictures to me and my mum of the drawings he'd done at school.

Harvey always likes to be in control of a situation. So at school, he made sure everybody knew he hated the doors banging. He had them wrapped around his little finger. They even had signs around the whole school saying, 'Please shut the doors quietly.' But that didn't stop him from kicking off. He once smashed all the windows in his classroom and he kicked down the emergency exit door on many occasions.

It's very rare he would ever go for anyone, like another pupil. It's usually just objects that are in Harvey's firing line. But that can be really dangerous for the other children around him.

There were 145 pupils at the school and Harvey had the worst behaviour, but he was one of the most able pupils. A lot of his peers were wheelchair-bound, so there'd be lots of children who weren't able to get out of the way if Harvey did flip and throw a chair or something. A lot of autistic children can be stronger than they look, and when they lose it, they really lose it. Everyone has different ways of calming him down. The school was very good at that.

Because Harvey was the most able there, it made it very difficult for him to make friends, as a lot of the students weren't able to communicate. And the friends he did have lived too far away for him to be able to see them outside of school.

Harvey likes to know exactly what is going to happen and when it's going to happen. So at school, he had a timetable which detailed all of the time slots for his lessons. His autism means he enjoys things being quite regimented.

People might be quite surprised that they actually do proper lessons at school. They do English, maths, cooking, all the usual subjects that you'd expect. His English is really good. He likes to write a lot of stories and as he writes, he spells out the words. Sometimes he can find it difficult to communicate verbally, but he communicates really well by the way he writes.

But there's no doubt about it, his favourite subjects are definitely art and music. I think some people just assume that if you have complex needs like Harvey, you don't have any type of education and that you just go to school and don't do much. But he is more than capable of learning – he's sat exams and passed them all, and I've kept all of his certificates.

They're all practical exams, rather than theory. So it's not like he sits down and writes for hours in silence in an exam hall. For example, if it was a maths exam, the teachers would take lots of pictures and videos of him writing down his times tables and saying them out loud. He loves to practise his times tables at home – he's really good at them.

In his earlier years, Harvey was also taught Makaton, which is a type of sign language. Because he couldn't talk or communicate when he was younger, it really helped him express himself.

He could sign things like, 'I'm feeling angry,' so that we could understand his emotions. And the more he used his Makaton, the more he slowly started to say words. It's almost like it triggered his speech. He still uses it now. He uses it quite often when he says, 'Yes please,' or, 'Mummy.'

I also think it helps to calm him down, because I used to encourage him to do it when I could tell he was about to kick off. If I could see he was about to have a tantrum, I'd say, 'Harvey can use his Makaton,' and it would sometimes stop him from lashing out.

During Harvey's time at Linden Lodge, he definitely became a lot more confident and grew into the man he is today. In the beginning, he didn't really like to socialise and attend the school parties. He liked to keep himself to himself. But towards the end, he would venture out a lot more.

His one-to-one teacher was really good with him

because she used to push him to do things out of his comfort zone. Once Harvey says no, he means no, but she was very good at persuading him.

This year was his last year at school. He graduated in July and it was such an emotional day for me. They organised a proper graduation ceremony for the pupils and he was presented with a certificate to say he'd completed his education at the school. He wore a blue cap and robe – and he looked so grown up. He even did the classic graduation photo, where you throw your cap in the air. I was bursting with pride. It was a brilliant day and Harvey loved every minute of it.

While it was sad to see him leave, I know he's ready for his next adventure at college. It's now time for Harvey to become an adult.

Twelve

DEFYING THE ODDS

Harvey has had the odds stacked against him all of his life, but my God, he has beaten them all. In fact, he hasn't just beaten them, he's smashed them – just like half of the furniture in the house!

Who would have thought it? My little boy, who was told he wouldn't be able to walk or talk, can now do both – and everything in between.

It still amazes me that Harvey can see after we were told the bombshell news that he was blind at six weeks old. If we're in a car and we're going past a railway station, he'll say, 'Look, Mum. A train track.' Or if we go past a bridge, he'll say, 'Look at the bridge, Mum.' He can also recognise people walking towards him. He's still registered as blind, and I don't know how clear his vision is, but he can definitely see something – which is incredible.

I would love to know exactly what he can see. The only way you can get some kind of understanding of it is when he goes for eye tests at the hospital. He reads out the letters on the board and is given pictures to look at.

He can see things when they're close up. The font he reads on his computer and iPad is 48 point size, which is very big. That's why he holds his iPad so close to his eyes. It's probably quite fascinating for people who don't know him to see that, but I'm just so used to it.

He did have glasses when he was younger, which he was supposed to wear to help magnify things for him. But he absolutely hated them. He'd start kicking off if I made him put them on, so it wasn't worth it. He has one eye stronger than the other, his right eye is much clearer. He also has nystagmus, which is a condition where your eyes move constantly. It means that when he's looking at something, he has to turn his head because his eye is moving in another direction. I can't imagine how frustrating that must be for him, but I guess he doesn't know any different.

Sometimes I forget how restricted his vision is because he does so well at home. If you saw him walking around the house, you'd think that he could see perfectly fine. I'm like, 'Harv, can you please go upstairs and get Mummy's phone?' Or I'll say, 'Can you get me a glass of water please?' And he does it with ease.

I think people would be shocked at just how well he does. But it's as soon as we take him out of his comfort zone that he struggles. If we go out somewhere he's never been before, he takes very light steps on the ground. He can't see where he's walking properly, so he likes to hold on to me. He can become quite clingy when we go to an environment he isn't used to.

I know for a fact that Harvey would never be able to just go out to the shops on his own, as he'd always have to have someone with him. I recently took him to some log cabins for a weekend away. It was dark one night and there was a really muddy hill next to our cabin. Poor Harvey – his little foot slipped and he fell over and rolled backwards. It was so heartbreaking to see.

He couldn't get himself up, but he was still holding his bloody iPad and charger in the air. He managed to save them in the fall, didn't he?! Honestly, that iPad is his whole life. It never leaves his hands. I did feel for him, though. His leg was twisted and he was shouting, 'Help.' It's really horrible seeing him vulnerable like that.

I'm not a believer in magic or voodoo, or anything like that. But I'll never forget the story I'm about to tell you. It freaks me out a little bit.

When Harvey was a baby, as I've said, I took him to work with me all the time. I was appearing on *Richard & Judy* and I had him in the green room with me along with my mum. Uri Geller was also on the show that day, so we were backstage with him.

We naturally got chatting and we were speaking about Harvey. I told him all about what we'd been through and that he was blind. I remember him saying to me, 'Let me do something with Harvey. I can guarantee that one day he will see.' I was thinking, 'What are you on about? What a load of bullshit!' We'd been told by doctors that he was blind and he will never be able to see, so why did this guy think he could perform a miracle? Did he think he was Jesus or something?

But I just thought, 'What's the worst that can happen? Go for it.' He asked a member of the film crew to go and get a spoon from the kitchen so that he could perform his infamous 'spoon bending' stunt.

He started rubbing the spoon and it started bending right in front of my eyes. I was like, 'What the hell is going on?!' He then said to me, 'Keep this spoon. I don't know when, but one day your son will see.'

And now, Harvey obviously does. Now, I'm not saying it's anything to do with Uri Geller. But when you look at Harvey's medical records, his eyes have not changed at all since he was a baby. They're exactly the same. He has no optic nerve, so how can he now see? We have absolutely no idea.

Whenever we take him to Moorfields Eye Hospital, they're fascinated that he's able to. It's so weird. Was it Uri Geller? Or was it because my mum and I had tried to stimulate his eyes from a young age? Or was it just a coincidence? Who knows. Make of it what you will!

Harvey has had so many amazing life experiences and met so many incredible people – and he doesn't even realise it.

In 2007, he even met the Queen. What an unbelievable opportunity that was. We went along to the opening of the Richard Desmond Children's Eye Centre, which is part of Moorfields Eye Hospital. It was such a special day because Harvey has been going to Moorfields since he was born.

I'm not normally phased by anyone – I don't get starstruck or anything like that. But when it comes to the Queen, it's a different story. She had such an aura about her. We all lined up and she came over and greeted us all and shook our hands.

Harvey was in his wheelchair and before the event, I had taught him to say, 'Hello, your Majesty.' He said it at exactly the right moment. I was so proud of him. He can be very unpredictable, so I was just so relieved he didn't swear at the Queen!

I spoke to her and told her how Harvey had been at Moorfields since day one, and how he could now see shapes and colours. She seemed genuinely interested in what I was saying and she was asking lots of questions about Harvey, which was nice.

Harvey has advanced so much from just seeing shapes and colours. He can draw amazing pictures on his iPad. I bought him a pen to go with it, but he won't use it. He just does it all with his fingers. He uses different parts of his fingers to create different lines and textures and he knows all the colours. It's amazing to watch. He's so good at drawing and it's always symmetrical. He can draw much better than anyone I know. I can't even remember how old he was when he first started drawing, but it's always been his favourite subject throughout school.

He draws lots of pictures of the family. He's actually quite good at drawing pictures of me. He captures the big boobs, big lips and long hair perfectly! He also sometimes takes pictures on his iPad and then draws over the top of them. For example, he'll take a picture of a train and then he'll use his finger to colour in the front of the train.

It really does blow my mind. We had so many doctors telling us that he definitely couldn't see, so it just goes to show that sometimes even the experts get it wrong.

As well as being fantastic at drawing, Harvey also has

an amazing musical talent. He loves playing the keyboard – he's like a little Stevie Wonder! He taught himself how to play from a young age, and he's loved it ever since. He likes to play nursery rhymes, like *Row, Row, Row Your Boat*. But he changes the word 'crocodile' to 'frog' and says, 'If you see a froggy, don't forget to ribbit.'

If Harvey has listened to something once, he can remember it. He has a really good understanding of rhythm. He can just make up a musical piece on the spot. I don't know how he does it.

He also loves listening to music. He's always been massively into his R&B. He loves Usher, Jay-Z and Drake. But his favourite song at the moment is *1 Thing* by Amerie. Sometimes I go on his iPad to look at all the drawings he's done and I've come across videos he's recorded of himself dancing to Amerie. He is very funny.

Last year, Harvey took part in Autism's Got Talent, which is run by the charity Anna Kennedy Online. It allows adults and children with autism to showcase their hobbies and interests. There are some really talented kids and it shows that autism is no barrier to success.

Harvey played his keyboard in front of a live audience and he was brilliant. I obviously would never force him to do something like that, but I asked him if he'd like to do it and he was so excited. But when we got there, it was a different story. He was kicking off backstage and he kept saying he didn't want to do it. He was having a full-on meltdown. So instead, we sat in the audience and watched the show.

While we were watching other people on stage, Harvey saw someone else playing the keyboard, so he chirped up a bit then and decided he did want to have a go at it after all. I brought him up onto the stage and as soon as he got up there he loved it. That's the trouble with Harvey, there's always an anticipation about how he's going to react.

He played *When The Saints Go Marching In*, and he was amazing. He really got the crowd going. He got a standing ovation. Harvey is not shy at all. When there's an audience and a microphone, he just takes over. He kept saying, 'Hello, everyone!' into the microphone. He knows exactly how to play a crowd – but I did have to warn him beforehand not to swear!

If he's in the right mood, Harvey is up for any challenge. We once went on holiday to the Maldives and I took him scuba diving. Never in a million years would I think he could do that – and I bet people are surprised to hear he can.

They make you practise in a big pool beforehand, and he did it all really well. He even learnt all the hand symbols they teach you so that you can communicate while you're under the water. If I asked Harvey now, he would still know what each of the symbols mean. He loved it. He probably found it quite easy after being taught sign language from a young age.

He loves all the water sports and activities you can do on holiday. He especially loves going on those big inflatable rubber rings that are attached to speedboats. I went on one with him once – and I'll never go on one again. I thought he was going to crush me!

He's always been an active boy. He used to love horse riding, swimming, trampolining and even quad biking. He still loves swimming – he's actually a really good swimmer. But it's quite worrying because when he's in the sea, he swims so far out. He has no concept of danger, so I have to keep a close eye on him and call him back in. If it was up to him, he would just swim and swim and swim!

Harvey may be 19 and excelling in life, but he's still a big baby at heart. His favourite time of the year is Christmas – he absolutely loves it. He's loved it since he was a baby. I think a lot of it has to do with the sensory side of it because of all the Christmas lights.

My mum always used to take him to garden centres during the festive period because they do the best lights. Although he couldn't talk at the time, we could just tell by his facial expression that he loved looking at the twinkling lights on the Christmas trees. We still take him to garden centres every year.

Harvey believes in Santa Claus and he writes a letter to him every year with a list of the presents he wants. Last year, it was a *Barney: Animal ABCs* DVD, a train toy that says 'all aboard', colouring pens and a new computer. You can get an app where Santa rings you and sends you a special message. So I organised that for him and he absolutely loved it. I could see him getting really giddy when Santa read out all the presents that Harvey had asked for.

And then he was told that he'd made Santa's nice list and he started rocking his body and making noises. Whenever he does that, it means he's very excited. He listened to that message on repeat for the next few weeks – which became very annoying!

But one thing Harvey doesn't like at Christmas is the sound of the paper being ripped off the presents. He also doesn't understand that receiving presents stops at some point. I have to explain you can't be opening presents all day long, one after another, and that you only get a certain amount to open. He opens one and then he's like, 'Next.' He doesn't get the concept of it at all.

He's also really difficult to buy for. I'd say he's the hardest child to pick presents for because my other kids go through all their presents and happily go up to their rooms and play, whereas Harvey is particular with what he likes. He tends to get a lot of crayons and pens as everyone knows he loves drawing. But I also try to get him practical things, like a new pair of trainers or some new clothes.

And I can't even count how many iPads I've bought him. The thing is, it's not just as simple as getting a new iPad. It has to be an iPad Pro with a black border. There are loads of different versions and colours, and if it's different to what he wants, he won't be happy. He once kicked off in the middle of a John Lewis store because they didn't have the specific one he wanted.

As I mentioned, Harvey now has his own house. He moved in earlier this year to help him become a bit more independent. I always imagined he would be with me forever, so that was such a big moment for me. I never thought he'd come this far. If I'm not there, he does have a carer staying with him, because he could never be left on his own.

I could leave him in the house for about two minutes to pop to the shops, but I'd have to be on FaceTime with him. He also has cameras in the house so that I can keep an eye on him. He has a huge bed, and he has toys on his bedside cabinets, like Barney the dinosaur. He bloody loves Barney. It's a three-bedroom house and I have my own bedroom there, so I can stay with him whenever I need to. Where he lives, there's an ice-cream man that comes to the street, and Harvey recognises the tune instantly. I'm always like, 'Please don't hear it, please don't hear it.' But he does – every single time. He says, 'Look Mum, the ice-cream van.' And he gets all excited and then I have to buy him an ice cream. He even knows that the man's name is Steve!

I'm currently in the middle of moving back to my house in Horsham – also known as the 'Mucky Mansion', thanks to the press. I'm having it all done up, and I'm also building Harvey his own place next to the house. He can't have a bedroom in the house because he just smashes it up. I have to think of his own safety and everyone else's safety.

So, he's going to have his own little safe haven. I'm basically designing it so that it's perfect for an adult with autism. He'll have padded walls again like he did when he was younger, he'll have his own safe kitchen and a huge water room with a big shower. It just needs to be somewhere that he can't smash up and somewhere that is easy to clean down. Obviously, he's at college, but it will be for whenever he comes home.

Another monumental moment for me was when Harvey turned 18, which meant he officially became an adult. On your 18th birthday, you usually spend it going to the pub with your mates, getting drunk, and avoiding your embarrassing mum! But because of Harvey's disabilities, his 18th party was far from that. Harvey has the mental age of a seven-year-old, so he wanted a tropical frog theme in the garden with the family. It was a perfect day for him and I wouldn't have wanted it any other way. I'm so proud of the man he's become and he has such good banter.

He doesn't realise just how funny he actually is. He comes out with the most hilarious things and sometimes I have no idea where he gets it from. We were once driving in the car and we had the window down because it was a hot day. A police car came zooming past us out of nowhere with the siren on. It made Harvey jump and he said, 'Fucking c***ing police.' Only Harvey would be able to get away with that!

He doesn't really know what he's saying – it's the context he says it in that makes me laugh. Harvey has lots of funny one-liners. One of my personal favourites is 'Oh, what a day!' I've seen online companies selling T-shirts with Harvey's sayings across the front, which is amazing. But I'm now thinking I should jump on it and get it copyrighted and earn Harvey some cash!

I actually had a company that sells celebrity video messages approach me about Harvey because they've had so many requests from people wanting a personalised video from him. Although I think it would be a great money earner for Harvey, I'm not sure if it's something I want him to do. It's a tricky situation. I think a lot of people would say I'm exploiting him, but you have to remember he is an adult – he's 19 now.

He gets recognised everywhere we go. Out of all my kids, Harvey and Princess are the ones who always get stopped when we're out. Sometimes I want to be in disguise and just lay low, but I've got no chance if Princess and Harvey are with me.

People just come up to Harvey and ask for pictures. When his school used to take him out on trips, I had to warn them that he does get recognised wherever he goes, so they should be prepared for people approaching them.

I let Harvey decide whether he wants to take a picture. If he doesn't, he's not afraid to tell them. You just don't know what is going to come out of his mouth. Sometimes he's extremely polite and he'll say hello to people, or other times he'll say something like, 'Hello you dickhead.' Thankfully, people know Harvey and know what he's like. They can laugh it off and he gets away with it.

But there are kids like Harvey who aren't in the public eye, who might look fine on the outside, but they could say something like, 'Fuck off you c***.' I've read about people with autism getting beaten up because people think they're just abusing them, which is horrendous.

I would be horrified if anyone ever laid their hands on Harvey. If someone hit him, he would cry like a baby. If you even just flicked him he would cry. Sometimes

I just muck around with him and we play-fight. He'll shout, 'No, Mum!' He's a big softie. Although he does love me pushing him onto the bed and tickling his belly, knees, elbows and under his chin. He goes into hysterical laughter. He holds his breath and I have to tell him to calm down and breathe.

I know I'm biased, but Harvey really is so special. He amazes me every day. He's done more things than I could ever have imagined. In fact, he's done more things than most able 19-year-olds have done.

We're fighting for a law in his name, he's an ambassador for the UK's leading learning disability charity, Mencap, he's got his own BBC documentary *Harvey And Me,* and we're currently filming the second instalment, *What Harvey Did Next.* He was even nominated for a National Television Award – more on that later – and he was shortlisted for Celebrity Of The Year at the National Diversity Awards for his charity work. Not bad, eh?!

Harvey has been used to the cameras ever since he was a baby because he was on all of my reality shows. He now understands that he's on TV, but when he was younger he wasn't aware of being filmed. I did question whether or not I should put Harvey on TV, but then I thought, 'Why shouldn't I?'

I didn't question whether my other children should be on my shows, so why should he be treated differently?

I think it's helped raise awareness about bringing up children who have disabilities, and people often thank me for doing so.

He's done a few live television appearances. His first was when he was six. I took him on *This Morning* with me for an interview with Phillip Schofield and Fern Britton. It was the first time I'd done an interview solely about Harvey. I thought viewers would be able to get a better understanding of his disabilities if he was with me. I've lost count of how many TV interviews I've done in the past, but I was really anxious about this one because I had no control of what might happen.

He's so unpredictable. Even just getting him from the car into the studio was a nightmare. But he was very well behaved while we were on air. He was happy playing with his ruler. I just wanted to go on and show what life was like with a disabled child and prove you should never feel ashamed or alone – and I think I did that.

We returned to the *This Morning* sofa eight years later, this time with my mum, too. I think everybody could see just how far he'd come. As we chatted to hosts Ruth Langsford and Eamonn Holmes, I asked Harvey, 'You do play up for Mummy sometimes don't you, Harv?' He replied, 'Yeah, babe!' I had no idea where that came from. That was the first time he'd used that word. And now he says it all the time!

He's got such a cheeky personality. When Eamonn was reading out lovely messages from the viewers, Harvey was saying, 'I love it!' It's nerve-racking taking him on live TV as I do worry about what he could say, as I experienced a year later during our infamous *Loose Women* appearance, but I never want to hide him away. Harvey loves going on TV and he loves watching himself back. Even now, he goes on YouTube and he'll watch clips of himself on *This Morning* and *Loose Women.*

I know Harvey doesn't really understand, but despite all of his challenges, he's a lucky boy. So many doors have been opened for him – and I know there's still so much more to come.

Thirteen

ON THE RIGHT TRACK

I bloody *hate* trains. If I never see another train again, I'll be honest, I won't be sad. But actually, that's a bit of a lie because trains are Harvey's passion. I hate them, but they make Harvey very happy – so I definitely have a love-hate relationship with them.

In fact, I can't believe I'm dedicating a whole chapter to trains. But I couldn't write a book about Harvey and not talk about trains, could I? When I explained to Harvey that I was writing a book about Harvey and Mummy, I asked him what he thought I should talk about. He, of course, said trains. I'm not sure why I bothered asking because I could have guessed the answer!

Harvey just sits and watches videos of trains on his computer all day long. It's all day, every day, and that's no exaggeration. It drives me bloody mad. I don't know when his obsession first started. For as long as I can remember, Harvey has loved trains.

Apparently it's a really common interest among people with autism. They say it's because trains meet many sensory needs – they're bright and colourful and have spinning wheels. Learning train schedules and train numbers can also be really relaxing for someone with autism. That's exactly what Harvey does.

He likes to memorise all the different timetables. If we're at a station and a train arrives, I'll ask him where it's going, and he can tell me straight away. 'It's going to Cambridge, Mum.' It's like he has an encyclopedic knowledge of trains.

When he draws pictures of trains, he includes every single detail. He knows all the colours of all the different trains and he even includes the train numbers – and they're actually the real numbers, he doesn't just make them up. It's really impressive.

Harvey likes to mimic the train announcements and he'll make us all sit and listen to him.

'May I have your attention please. Platform four will be the 11.10 service to London Bridge. This train is formed of 12 coaches. Please do not leave cases or parcels unattended anywhere in the station. Any items are likely to be removed without warning.'

I think I now subconsciously know every single train that leaves every single station, its train number and its departing and arrival time. I can probably even recite the rhythm of the train tracks. Thanks, Harv!

While most 19-year-olds are in nightclubs, Harvey's favourite thing to do is to visit the local train station. It's definitely not my idea of fun, but if it makes him happy, then it makes me happy. We stand at the platform and just wait for the trains. When he can hear them coming, he says, 'Can you hear the train, Mum?' I'm like, 'Yes, Harv. It's hard to miss it!' They're so bloody loud.

His face lights up when they come past and he takes about 100 photos of them – and he likes to show me every single one! The camera roll on his iPad is just picture after picture of trains. And then he has to delete them all because he uses up all of his memory! When we leave he waves and usually says something along the lines of, 'Bye train. Have a nice time. Love you.'

I recently took him to a station which has an old train carriage on the track, but he started sulking because it wasn't moving. I thought he would have loved it because he could get up close to it and touch it and take all the photos he wanted. But no – apparently it's only trains in service that he likes. He's very particular.

But he's not fussy when it comes to the train companies. He loves them all – Great Western Railway, Southern Railway, Thameslink and Greater Anglia. You name it, he loves it. But his favourite is the Gatwick Express. I organised a family day on the Gatwick Express for Harvey a couple of years ago. Junior and Princess came along with us, too. I can't say it was the most exciting day, but as long as Harvey had a good time, that's all that mattered.

The train manager kindly announced over the tannoy that Harvey Price was on board. As you can imagine, it made Harvey very excited. He was given a certificate with his name on to remind him of the journey and they made him his own personalised lanyard. He was also invited to sit at the front of the train with the driver, which he absolutely loved.

When he was 16, Harvey was lucky enough to have his artwork put up at Gatwick Station. The station manager saw his drawings on Instagram and contacted me about getting a picture blown up to put on the wall. We all went along as a family to see it get unveiled. That was the first of many amazing opportunities.

After *Harvey And Me* aired, lots of people saw how much he loves trains. Train companies got in touch with me and offered Harvey free tickets to go wherever he liked with his friend Zack. Network Rail also asked if Harvey would like to record his very own announcement for the trains at one of their stations. He's now also landed his own eight-part train series. How cool is that? Maybe 'cool' isn't the right word, but it's cool for Harvey. It'll follow him and his friend Zack and their love for trains. I think that's Harvey's dream job right there.

With his school, he recently did some work experience at Clapham Junction station. So maybe he could get a job in the future doing something that involves trains. Who knows? He's actually recently been offered another paid job to open up three train stations. He's not doing too shabby. He's going to have more money than his mum soon!

The funny thing is, all Harvey wants to spend his money on is carrot cake and felt-tip pens. Harvey has so many pens. I swear, if I got all his pens together it would fill up his whole bedroom. Every time I call at the supermarket I have to bring back pens for Harvey. But they have to be a certain brand that he likes. If I get him the wrong ones, he's not happy.

Harvey's second love in life is frogs. I think it's a very close runner-up to trains. Again, he's been fascinated by frogs for as long as I can remember. Whenever he's excited, he'll say, 'Ribbit ribbit.' His impression of a frog is actually very good.

His favourite frogs are bullfrogs – I personally didn't even know there were different types of frogs. He loves anything frog-related and his favourite colour is green. He has a frog-eyed headband, which he loves wearing. And he has a pair of Adidas Kermit The Frog trainers. He calls them his 'froggy trainers' and he never takes them off.

Harvey's birthdays usually involve a frog-themed party with a frog cake. On his 17th birthday, I even dressed up as a giant frog for him. The things us mums do for our children!

The thing with Harvey is, he loves frogs, but it's more so pictures of frogs rather than *actual* frogs. I found a woman who had loads of exotic frogs and I arranged for her to come to the house as I thought it would be brilliant for Harvey. The frogs were all different colours and I knew that he'd love it.

She got them all out and lined them all up for Harvey to look at. He kept going up close to them and saying, 'Wow!' And then she gave him the chance to hold one – and he chucked it across the room.

Oh my God! I couldn't believe it. That poor woman and her poor frog! I was absolutely mortified. Thankfully, the frog was okay, but I don't think the woman was. I think Harvey almost gave her a heart attack. Harvey threw it because in his head, he thought it would make the frog start hopping and making 'ribbit' noises. Let's just say he won't be going that close to an actual real-life frog again.

Since then, we've shown him frogs – from a very safe distance – but he doesn't seem that bothered about them. Jett and Bunny love the outdoors. I call them feral kids because they're not afraid to get dirty, which I love. So they often find frogs and pick them up and put them in buckets to show Harvey. But Harvey prefers to stick to the cartoon frogs on his iPad – I think that's best for everyone's sake!

Fourteen

AMY

Harvey has such a special bond with my mum. Everything he does is for his nanny. If he draws a picture, the first person he'll want to show is Nanny. Or if he's taken a video on his iPad, he'll send it straight to her. She's been with us through thick and thin and I probably don't tell her enough, but I appreciate everything she does for both of us.

I've spoken so much about my mum in this book and how much of an amazing help she's been, so I wanted her to have her own chapter so that she could talk about life with Harvey in her own words and from her perspective.

But first, let me tell you a little bit about my relationship with my mum. We've always been extremely close. I know everyone says this about their mum, but she really is the best mum in the world. She's very loving and protective, and she will do anything for her children and grandchildren. She's the first person I'd turn to in a crisis. She has taught me everything I need to know about being a mum.

I have nothing but fond memories of my childhood. We had a very stable family life growing up. As a kid, I was a bit of a tomboy and it was all about getting out in the fresh air. I loved riding my bike and playing out with my friends. And I was obsessed with my horses.

As I said earlier, my biological dad walked out on us and left my mum. I was only young and it didn't affect me, but it must have been really tough for my mum. I now know exactly what it's like being abandoned by the father of your child.

But my mum is strong and independent – and she definitely taught me that resilience. My mum has always supported me in any situation. She's been with me through all the trauma and all the heartache, but also all the good times. She's been a rock for me throughout my whole life.

But in 2017 it was my turn to be a rock for her. That was when she was diagnosed with the terminal lung condition idiopathic pulmonary fibrosis, also known as IPF, and given a life expectancy of three to five years.

So, if you do the maths, time is running out. When I

first found out, I was in bits. I felt like my whole world had been torn apart. Plus, just a week before her diagnosis, my marriage to Kieran had ended. So it was a really difficult time in my life.

I couldn't stay off Google. I became obsessed with Googling the condition and reading other people's stories – and that's the worst thing you can do. But you can't help it, it's just human instinct. We all do it because we want to know answers. But you see all kinds of things on Google and there's a lot of conflicting opinions and advice. And usually, you just look at the worst, which doesn't make you feel any better.

I actually didn't see my mum for a few weeks after we found out because I just physically felt like I couldn't. She couldn't understand why I wasn't going to visit her, but I couldn't face seeing her knowing that she was going to die. I thought that if I avoided her, I could try and blank out the reality of what was going on.

I couldn't stop crying. I'm not much of a crier, I usually put a wall up and just deal with things. And if I do cry, it's always in private. But when I appeared on *Loose Women* in December of that year I broke down. I was speaking about my mum and I just couldn't hold in the tears. TV presenter Keith Chegwin had just died of the condition – and that really brought it home for me. I'd read stories on Google about people dying of the condition, but when it happens to someone you know, it suddenly feels very real.

I did *Celebrity Big Brother* with Keith and we were actually in touch with him just a few weeks before his death. He gave my mum loads of advice about IPF. I was just so terrified about losing my mum. I ended up having to walk off the show because it all got too much for me.

At first, all we were told was that she had IPF and it was terminal. Hearing the word 'terminal' is horrendous. The scariest part is the thought of the unknown. We didn't know if she had weeks, months or years. I couldn't bear the thought of not seeing her grow old and her not being around to see Harvey grow and develop – and the rest of the kids.

I had all these thoughts running through my head and all these fears about the future, so I can't even imagine how my mum was feeling. She's an extremely strong woman.

I know that she's accepted it, and even though I'm sure it's on her mind every day, she doesn't dwell on it. As I said, she's always been the complete opposite to me when it comes to things like that. Her attitude towards this illness has been the same as it was when we were told about Harvey's conditions. I suppose I'm a glass half empty kind of person and she's a glass half full.

But I've accepted it now because I have to. She has an

incurable disease and that's just the reality of it. I know it sounds awful, but once we knew the prognosis, I even spoke to my mum about her funeral and what she wants for it. I think it's much easier to organise a funeral if you know what they want.

But we try not to make it all doom and gloom. As a family, we're really good at making light of a situation, even if it's a shit situation. We do try to have a laugh. Laughter is the best medicine, after all. Every time she speaks about her illness, I tell her to put the violins away. I joke with her and say she should spend loads of money and run up some credit card debts because once she's gone they can't chase her for it.

There should be more awareness of the condition because I don't think many people know about it. Once you're diagnosed, unfortunately, there's nothing you can do. My mum had a continuous cough for about five years, but they just put it down to asthma in the beginning. She pushed for answers because her inhalers weren't working. Because of what we'd been through with Harvey, we knew that doctors can make mistakes and that you shouldn't always trust the first opinion.

She ended up going for an X-ray and that's when something showed up on her lungs. She was referred to a specialist and was given the diagnosis. Sophie and I were with her when she got the results. 'Just cut all the bullshit and tell us how long she's got left to live,' I said to the doctor. I know it's very blunt, but I didn't need to hear all the medical terms that didn't make any sense to us. I just wanted to know the facts.

She's always lived a healthy lifestyle and she doesn't smoke, so it's so unfair seeing her suffer. But as I know, life is unfair, isn't it? After going through everything that I have with Harvey, I know you can't take anything for granted.

Despite her illness, my mum still likes to keep fit. She's much more active than I am! Her illness is starting to slow her down, but she still likes to do her spinning classes every morning. If she didn't go to the gym, her lungs would seize up, so it's really good for her to stay active.

She's met other families through the British Lung Foundation and made some really good friends who are going through a similar situation. They meet up on Zoom and do their virtual fitness classes together. Whenever something like this happens, my mum has always been brilliant at researching charities and finding support groups. Without them, I don't know where we would be with Harvey.

When my mum started to struggle with her breathing, she moved to Spain for a few months because the cold weather over here was making her worse. The warm air was really good for her lungs. While she was over there, she was getting out and about and going for long walks. She was getting in about 10,000 steps a day, which is brilliant. It was hard not having her around, but she had to do what was right for herself.

Now, she's only got around 32 per cent of her lung capacity, whereas the average person has around 100 per cent. So you can imagine how out of breath she gets.

She gets tired easily too, so it's not like she can spend as much time with Harvey as she used to. She's now on oxygen as well. I found that hard to deal with because in my head, once you start on the oxygen, you kind of know what's coming next. Whenever she speaks, she coughs and gasps for air. But she's always reluctant to increase her oxygen levels because she doesn't like to rely on it.

It's heartbreaking to see her like that. But it doesn't stop her from nagging me! I'm such a chatterbox and I definitely get that from my mum. So now when she tries to talk, we're like, 'Shut up and save your energy!'

The last year has been really tough because we haven't been able to see her as much as we usually would. Obviously everyone has been affected by the Covid-19 pandemic and people all over the world have been separated from their loved ones. Because of her condition, my mum was extremely high-risk, so she had to shield to keep herself safe.

If she'd have caught coronavirus, it would have killed her. Even if she catches a common cold, it could be fatal for her. And it's the same with Harvey. He probably wouldn't have stood a chance if he had coronavirus. Harvey found it really difficult to understand why he couldn't see his nanny.

We went round to her garden to visit her from a distance a few times when it was safer, but Harvey kept wanting to go inside her house and give her a hug. He has no idea what coronavirus is. 'I hate this!' he would say, and he'd have a strop.

My mum is currently on a transplant list, so she could get a call any day. But we're not getting our hopes up. You basically have to be in a critical condition to be able to qualify for one, which seems stupid. Why wouldn't they give the transplant to someone who was a bit healthier and could cope with such a life threatening operation? It doesn't make any sense to me.

And even if she did have a transplant, it doesn't mean to say she'd survive it because your body can reject it and you can die on the operating table. Plus, it's not a cure. It only prolongs your life for an extra five years or so, if that.

I actually offered to give her one of my lungs because like most people, I would do anything for my mum. I thought it would just be easy to do, but it's very complicated. Even if it was an option, she wouldn't ever let me do that anyway.

If she doesn't get a transplant, she'll receive palliative care to make her as comfortable as possible in her final stages. I know every terminal illness is unpleasant, but it really is such a cruel way for her to go.

Her lungs have scarring on them, which is getting progressively worse every day. And then it will get to the point where she'll no longer be able to breathe at all. So she will basically suffocate. She's deteriorating rapidly. Every Christmas I just assume it could be her last one. I've learnt to spend as much time as I can with my mum. You've just got to take each day as it comes because that's all you can do. We build as many memories as we can as a family. We don't have regrets and we try to be happy.

My mum has always said that being with Harvey makes you appreciate everything that little bit more. Because of Harvey, I think my mum has done things in life she probably wouldn't have done otherwise. I suppose she felt like she wanted to give back. She's worked with a lot of charities over the years. She also once spent three months in India helping children in the slums.

My mum really is my inspiration. Her motto in life has always been, 'Feel the fear and do it anyway.' And I couldn't agree more.

Fifteen

A GRANDMOTHER'S LOVE

By Amy Price

I don't even know where to begin when it comes to describing Harvey, my first grandchild. When you have children, you think your heart couldn't get any fuller. And then a grandchild comes along and fills a hole you never knew was empty.

We're so lucky to have Harvey in our lives. I'm so proud of him and everything he's achieved. He's inspirational. He's got a lot against him, but he's still a cheerful and intelligent boy. I always call him a boy, but he hates that. He says, 'No Nan, I'm a man, not a boy.'

Harvey is just really good fun and an absolute joy to be around. He is very, very funny. He mimics a lot of my phrases. If you say to him, 'What does Nanny say?' He'll go, 'Ooooh.'

He loves showing me his drawings. He makes sure that he gives Katie all of the drawings he's done to pass on to me if I don't see him. I always used to encourage him with his artwork and I'd always give him praise because he absolutely loves praise. If you tell him he's done a good job at something, he gets very excited.

Harvey also knows his limits. For example, if I ask him to do something and he doesn't want to do it, he'll say, 'No, thank you.' Once he's decided he doesn't want to do something, he won't do it.

I can't believe how fast the years have gone. Going back to the very beginning, I remember it was such an exciting time when Katie told us she was pregnant. I was a little bit shocked, but I was absolutely thrilled.

I knew Katie would make a fantastic mum, but I was also a bit concerned because she was so young and there was a lot going on with Dwight. Their relationship was unstable to say the least. I don't think he was keen to have the baby, but Katie was determined and we were all right behind her.

When she broke up with Dwight, she really wanted to get him involved in the pregnancy still. She was sending him books about babies and she'd send him all the pictures of the scans. But to be honest, he wasn't that interested. I think that hurt her a lot.

Katie was really well during the pregnancy and she was so excited about becoming a mum. She was waiting for her house to be ready at the time, so she moved in with me so that I could support her. We had a spare bedroom with an en suite for her and we helped get everything ready ahead of the baby arriving.

I was with her throughout the birth, as was her friend Sally. Katie brought some music with her to the hospital and she'd planned to play it throughout her labour, but in the end, she wanted it completely quiet.

The birth was quite horrific for her. I think she should have had a caesarean because he was bigger than they expected. Looking back, I don't know whether that could have played a part in causing the problems Harvey has today, but it's hard to say. You just don't know – and I guess we'll never know.

When Harvey arrived, it was like a bloodbath. I've never seen anything like it. I know you bleed after giving birth, but this was a lot of blood. I was so concerned that I actually called the nurse over and asked if it was normal. She reassured me it was completely normal, but it looked barbaric to me.

Dwight turned up at the hospital and he held Harvey.

He had him in his arms and he would take him up and down the hospital corridor. I must admit, at that time, he did seem quite taken with Harvey. But things soon turned sour.

When he asked Katie for a DNA test because he thought Harvey's skin was too light for him to be his, she was absolutely devastated. That really did upset her – and it upset us as a family. We were all really affected by it. It was really cruel.

She was going through heartache, but Katie was over the moon with Harvey and he kept her strong. She really was completely smitten. It was so lovely to see.

He seemed to be a really good baby, but as we look back, that's because he wasn't well. When Harvey was six weeks old, things changed dramatically. That's when a doctor at the Ear, Nose And Throat department told us he was blind. It was devastating.

I think we were both upset separately, but never together. We put on a brave face because we felt like we wanted to be strong for each other.

After we were told, we went straight home and we were just standing in the kitchen feeling a bit lost. We said to each other, 'Well, that's it then. What are we going to do now?' And we just got on with it. That's how we pursued it, really. We just had to deal with it. We even got a second opinion from an eye specialist in America, just to be sure. We were told Harvey was definitely blind, but I always had hope.

Harvey was also sleeping and eating a lot. And when I say a lot, I mean *a lot*. In the night, he would drink 13 bottles of milk. He was growing bigger and bigger and in the end, I stopped working to help look after him because Katie just couldn't cope on her own. It wasn't a difficult decision for me at all. Like any mum, you want to do what's best for your children. I never had any regrets.

I'm so glad I did it because now, I can see the rewards from all that time I spent with him. Harvey loves music and he loves swimming – and I like to think I played a part in that. He loved music from a young age. He used to drive me mad in the car because he constantly wanted to sing nursery rhymes. He also had lots of instruments, which he used to throw out of the car window half of the time! It was hard work, but it was all worth it because I really believe it developed him.

I did some research to see if there was anywhere we could take Harvey to get some support and I found Blatchington Court in Brighton, who have helped us ever since. They actually helped us get Harvey into his new residential college, National Star, so we've come a long way with them.

They held coffee mornings for families with blind and partially sighted children and there, we were introduced to three mums. It was so nice to speak to other people who were going through a similar situation. We used to meet up with them once a week and they would often say to us that they thought Harvey could have diabetes insipidus because he was a big baby and he was drinking a lot. We shut them down because we trusted what the doctors had told us.

But to be honest, the doctors at the Royal Sussex County Hospital didn't really seem to have a clue what to do with Harvey because his condition was so rare. The mums really pushed us to get referred to Great Ormond Street and that's when we saw Dr Dattani, who diagnosed Harvey instantly and started him on the right medication.

Dr Dattani also referred us to a doctor at Moorfields Eye Hospital called Professor Moore. We made an appointment with him and I can remember the day so clearly. When he saw Harvey, he held up a mosaic glass elephant and Harvey looked straight at it. It was amazing. He told us that Harvey did have some sight, although he couldn't be sure of exactly how much. But he explained we could try and work on it and see what we could do to help Harvey.

We went from being told that he was definitely blind and there was nothing they could do, to this doctor telling us the complete opposite. I've always told people to keep getting another opinion if you have your doubts.

Don't always stick with the first one, or even the second one, because they might be wrong. It was very relieving to hear because it gave us both a bit of hope.

Katie always used to say to me, 'Will he ever be able to talk? Will he ever be able to walk? Will he ever be able to cuddle me?' And I always told her that he would. I was sure of it. Up until the age of four or five, he didn't really talk at all, but I knew he would in the end.

With all of his complex needs, Harvey is very intelligent. He's not stupid at all. I always knew something was there, it was just a case of trying to develop him. One moment that really struck me was when Harvey got his first iPad. I downloaded a game for him which was a bit like matching pairs – and he could do it instantly. He was only young at the time. I thought, 'Blimey!' I was very impressed. I knew that something was going on with him somewhere, we just had to channel it and get it out.

We then started taking Harvey for drop-in sessions at Dorton House, the school for blind and visually impaired children. We still didn't know exactly what sight he had, so they gave us tips on how we could try and stimulate his eyes. They told us to make a baby mobile with CDs because the light catches on it, or to shine a torch under a blanket to try and get Harvey to look at the light. I was determined that we would help in any way we could.

We then started to notice a few behavioural problems

with Harvey. He used to throw himself back and have tantrums. He wouldn't eat properly because he didn't like sticky or soft things – he became very particular. And he also had a problem with noise. He didn't like the sound of cutlery clashing or doors banging. It's because he couldn't see, so sudden noises used to frighten him. He's still like that now, which is why he wears ear defenders. We didn't realise at the time, but we later got told that he's on the autistic spectrum.

He started at Dorton House full-time, and that's when he really started to develop and come out of his shell. I used to take him there in the car every day myself. It shut down when he was 11, which was such a shame. It was a really good school and we thought he was going to go all the way through there.

After that, he went to Linden Lodge. It was very hard to find a school for Harvey nearby that could cater to his needs because he's so complex. It was in Wimbledon, so a driver would take him to school every day and I went along with him for the first year.

I looked after Harvey for about 14 years, but I had to stop in the end because he got so big and I couldn't handle him on my own.

Some of the journeys in the car to school were really hard. If he didn't want to go to school, it would be an impossible task trying to get him in the car. And then sometimes he'd kick off and try to hit the driver. I would be in the back with him trying to pacify him, but as he got bigger and bigger, I just couldn't do it any more. It was too much for me because he became unpredictable and he's very strong.

But I still helped out with what I could and even now, I keep on top of all of Harvey's hospital appointments because Katie can be bloody useless! She's got so much going on that she forgets a lot of stuff. So whenever the hospital sends her emails, they make sure to copy me in so that I can remind her.

I sit in with her on a lot of the Zoom meetings as well. The hospitals have all been amazing with Harvey – especially Great Ormond Street and Maudsley Hospital. Because he has so many different things wrong with him, he's on so much medication. Each of his conditions have to be closely monitored and they have to constantly tweak his medication to get the right balance, which can be tough. Once he does have the right balance, it really helps. And then it means that when he's being naughty, it's just because he's a naughty boy – it's not down to his condition.

Harvey can definitely pull the wool over our eyes. He's not daft, put it that way! For example, if he wants a cake and Katie tells him he can't have one, he'll wait until she's out of the room and he'll say to me, 'Can I have a cake,

Nan?' He can play you. He's not stupid by any means. He can be crafty.

Katie used to have to lock the door in the kitchen because he'd constantly go into the fridge and take food without her noticing. But a lot of the time he used to find the key anyway and just help himself. He'd take frozen pizzas out of the freezer and hide them under his bed. He puts food here, there and everywhere! He would get up in the night when everyone was asleep and raid the fridge. Because of his Prader-Willi syndrome, he never feels full. And because of his diabetes insipidus, he can't control how much he drinks. So for Harvey, he's hungry and thirsty all the time and that's the problem. I can't imagine how that must feel for him.

Harvey is an innocent, loving boy and it shocks me how anyone could say anything cruel about him. The trolling Harvey gets is really hurtful for Katie – and for all of us. Some of the things I've read are absolutely terrible. We got to the point where we were just completely fed up with it. Katie said, 'We need to do something about this.' And that's when we started the petition and pushed for Harvey's Law. It was all Katie's idea and I just helped her.

It was incredible to get the opportunity to go to the House of Commons and speak to MPs about our experience. We've now also set up Track A Troll and we're working hard to try and make it law that someone has to give proof of their identity when setting up a social media account. It's very hard to get people to listen.

I know they're currently trying to get social media companies to take responsibility and to police their websites, but the laws need to be updated and changed. People need to be punished. Harvey can't defend himself, so we'll never stop fighting for him and for everyone else.

Katie and Harvey have a special, special bond. It's a maternal instinct where she just wants to protect him. Anyone who has a child with a disability knows that you give that little bit more because you have to. Their relationship is more than 100 per cent. To Harvey, Katie is his whole world. And of course Katie's children are her whole world.

I think it's sad that Dwight isn't in Harvey's life. His agent has always been in contact with me. If Harvey isn't well, she'll message me and ask how he is. But Dwight never asks himself.

In 2020, Harvey was hospitalised and was really poorly in intensive care. Dwight's agent rang me and asked how bad he was. I said, 'Look, this has got to stop now. If Dwight wants to know about Harvey, he's got our number and he should ring us himself.' He shouldn't be going through his agent. It's about time he took some responsibility. But we've heard nothing from Dwight, which is a shame. Harvey is also missing out on a relationship with his brother, as Dwight has another son. It really is such a shame because we always had a good relationship with Dwight.

In my opinion, I think Pete being with Katie interfered a lot when it came to Dwight's relationship with Harvey. Dwight and Pete never got on. Pete said he wanted to adopt Harvey and Dwight was shocked by that. I think one of the main reasons Dwight didn't visit Harvey at the house was because he felt uncomfortable around Pete. I also think Dwight found Harvey's disabilities confusing. He just couldn't understand why Harvey was so ill and why he had so many problems. I think he found it really hard to accept.

I genuinely don't think Harvey is bothered about Pete or Kieran because Katie is his everything.

Harvey has started college now and it's time for him to be a bit more independent. He likes having his own space because he doesn't like a lot of noise. When they're all together as a family, he says, 'I've had enough now. I want peace and quiet.' And he'll go off and find somewhere to sit on his own.

I'm hoping he'll develop a bit further at college and that they can really help him reach his full potential. I'm pretty certain he could hold down a job of some sort in the future, although I'm not sure exactly what kind of job. It would have to be a repetitive job because of his autism.

There's a possibility he might be able to work somewhere like a garden centre, or in a supermarket stacking shelves. Or maybe he'll even be able to have a career in music or design. The sky's the limit. Katie and I always used to disagree about his future, but I always used to tell her he'd be able to achieve anything.

Looking back at everything he's been through, he's come so far. Although I may not be around to see it, I know for certain his future is bright.

Sixteen

COMPLEX CONDITIONS

Harvey is perfect in every single way in my eyes, but as you know, he has many complex needs. While they're extremely challenging, thankfully, they are not life limiting as long as he continues to take his medication.

When I was first told that Harvey was blind all those years ago, it was the worst thing in the world. I felt like his whole life was over because he'd never be able to see. But now, I don't even worry about his eyes because I know he has some vision. It's his behaviour and weight that have become the most worrying things for me.

I've never been told that Harvey has a short life expectancy, but it's his weight that is the main concern.

As he's gotten older, he's become bigger and bigger. Now, my focus is really trying to help him lose weight because at 26 stone, it's putting a huge strain on his heart.

Throughout the book, I've mentioned Harvey's different conditions and how they affect him. But I thought it would be interesting, and hopefully educational, to go into them all in a bit more detail. The list is quite long, and it's constantly changing and getting updated. I am by no means a medical expert, but this is everything I know about Harvey's health.

Septo-optic dysplasia

Once we were told Harvey was blind, this was the first condition we knew he had. He was diagnosed by Dr Dattani at Great Ormond Street.

It's a condition that affects around one in every 10,000 births. It's defined by optic nerve hypoplasia, midline brain abnormalities and pituitary gland abnormalities. Usually, children with septo-optic dysplasia only have two of the three problems. One-third will have all three – which Harvey does.

So, to break it down into more simple terms, optic nerve hypoplasia means that the optic nerve has not developed properly during pregnancy and it remains small. This is why Harvey has visual impairment.

Midline brain abnormalities affect the part of the brain

that helps you to develop, so it causes a delay in reaching milestones. This was the reason Harvey couldn't walk or talk until he was older.

Finally, pituitary gland abnormalities basically means that his pituitary gland, which is the gland in the brain that produces hormones, doesn't work. It's a condition called panhypopituitarism. As his body is unable to produce a normal level of hormones, it can delay puberty. So I have to inject him with a growth hormone daily.

When Harvey was younger, we visited Dr Dattani every month for about six months to check his development. Dr Dattani had different-size testicle shapes on a ring and he would check them against Harvey to make sure he was developing correctly. Even to this day, Harvey refers to Dr Dattani as the 'balls doctor' as he remembers those appointments so clearly.

Having pituitary gland abnormalities also means that Harvey's body can't release cortisol – the essential hormone that kicks in in times of stress to give your body a boost.

We need much more cortisol than usual when suffering from stress. If Harvey falls over and really hurts himself or gets into a situation which has shaken him up, it can be fatal. It's known as primary adrenal insufficiency. It's very serious. So he has to be given an emergency hydrocortisone injection whenever that happens. That's why it's so worrying when something happens to him, like when he burned his leg in the bath.

More recently, Harvey spent five days in intensive care last year. He just wasn't himself and I knew he was ill because his breathing was really fast and his temperature was soaring. It was ridiculously high – it went up to 42 degrees.

It was a really dangerous situation for him to be in, so I phoned 999 and he was taken to Epsom General Hospital immediately. Usually when people are rushed to the hospital, they go straight to the emergency room, but Harvey went straight into the resuscitation room. The whole thing was a complete blur, but I just remember there were suddenly eight doctors standing around him.

It was exactly like something I'd seen in *Holby City*. It was terrifying. He's obviously been hospitalised in the past, but I'd never been in this situation with him before. He'd actually been in hospital just a couple of weeks before this. He was complaining of chest pains and it can be difficult with Harvey because he can't communicate how he feels properly.

I was asking him to describe how he felt and he kept saying that his chest felt like needles. So I instantly called an ambulance and he was taken in for checks. Everything came back clear. They suspected that it could be the start of a chest infection, so he was given some medicine and I was allowed to bring him home.

But I knew this time was very different. I genuinely feared he was dying. Because he was 18 and classed as an adult, the parents aren't usually allowed in the room. But obviously, you can't talk to Harvey like how you'd talk to anyone else, so I think they realised very quickly that I needed to be in the room with him.

I always say that I'm like Harvey's personal dictionary. I can tell the doctors about all the medication he has and I had to explain that he needed his emergency injection as soon as possible. He actually had to have the injection a total of four times because his body wasn't responding to it. I've never felt more scared in my life.

He was so ill. It was awful to see. The doctors were putting drips in his arms and like me, Harvey hates needles. He would usually kick off about it, but he was just laying there in silence letting them do it. It was horrible to see him covered in tubes.

Once they'd stabilised him, they took him into intensive care. He had no energy, but he still managed to shout out, 'I want my mummy.' It was heartbreaking. I felt completely helpless. And the worst thing was that no one knew what was wrong with him. They kept doing tests on him but they weren't getting any answers.

There were also very strict Covid restrictions at the

time, so I could only visit him within certain hours. I tried to keep myself as busy as I could, but I was just thinking the worst. Every time I shut my eyes at night I could just picture Harvey laying in the hospital bed with his body covered in tubes.

I got a lot of stick from people online asking me why I wasn't by Harvey's bedside 24/7, but I wasn't allowed to be. Trust me, I wanted to be. But I had to follow the rules. I was trying to take my mind off things by carrying on with my life and trying to keep everything as normal as possible at home.

Every time my phone rang, I was just expecting bad news. Those few days were torture. But thank God Harvey made a recovery. In the end, they said he had an infection in his body, but they didn't know exactly how he got it. They told me that my knowledge on the first day made a massive difference. It's lucky that I was there, otherwise it could have been a very different ending.

Diabetes insipidus

When Harvey was diagnosed with septo-optic dysplasia, he was also diagnosed with diabetes insipidus. Some people think this means he has diabetes, but he doesn't. When the pituitary gland has abnormalities, it can also cause other conditions, and this is one of them.

It's rare, affecting one in 25,000 people. It means he

needs to urinate more than the average person and has the constant feeling of extreme thirst. It can be hard to diagnose in young children because they can't speak and express how they feel, but as I mentioned earlier, Harvey was constantly drinking as a baby – and that's why. Other symptoms include high body temperature, which Harvey gets from time to time, and fatigue.

Autism

Out of all of Harvey's conditions, autism is the one I find the most difficult. Don't get me wrong, it makes him who he is, but it's hard bloody work. Autism is a spectrum, so everyone is different. But these are the signs Harvey has.

He gets very upset if he doesn't like a certain taste or sound – especially sound. As I've said, he absolutely hates loud, sudden noises. Hence why he hates doors banging. He also hates people sneezing. If you don't warn him that you're about to sneeze, he kicks off.

Harvey isn't as fussy with his food now, but he used to be. Like I mentioned, he went through a phase of only eating mini kievs and he had to have his toast cut into triangles. But if I give him his dinner and there's something on the plate he doesn't like, he refuses to eat the whole thing.

For example, if I make him some fish and chips and I accidentally put one pea on the plate, he will say, 'No thanks, Mum.' Or he'd pick up the pea and throw it across the room. Most people would just ignore the pea on the plate, but it really frustrates him. He's very particular. It's quite fascinating to see.

He also gets upset if I ask him to do something he doesn't want to do, but I guess that's like most teenagers. But Harvey's version of being upset isn't just going into a strop. Harvey being upset is extreme. It's chucking things across the room, headbutting things and punching and kicking the wall.

Harvey does a lot of repetitive movements, like rocking his body, flapping his hands or flicking objects – like a ruler or a coat hanger – really close to his eyes. When he flaps his hands, he likes to make the tune of a railway track. So he'll often do it on the table, or on an empty water bottle. It sounds exactly like a train chugging along the tracks – and he knows the exact rhythm of it.

Harvey is very verbal, but it's in his own little language. He also tends to repeat the same phrases. And not only does he repeat them, but I have to finish his sentences for him, too. If I say the wrong thing, which I do on purpose sometimes to wind him up, he gets so annoyed. If he says, 'Oh my' and I say back, 'Bananas?' He'll be like, 'No, Mum.' And if I don't answer him back he'll keep saying 'Mum?' I'll be like, 'What?' And he says, 'Please, Mum.' And I say, 'Okay, God.' And that makes him very happy.

Harvey also asks the same question over and over again. He mainly does that when he's out of his comfort zone, like if I take him shopping. He will constantly ask me, 'Where are we going?'

He also enjoys repeating the same activities, like watching a video multiple times. As you can imagine, that can be very annoying for anyone in his company! He's created his own tune on his iPad, and whenever we're in the car he'll play it on repeat. Everyone knows it – and everyone *hates* it. He zones out when he's listening to it and I have to say to him, 'Harv! Turn it down.'

When someone has autism, you have to try and teach them about emotions and that can be quite tricky. I know you have to teach all children about emotion, but I had to teach Harvey in a way that was very clear and straightforward.

Harvey can express how he feels now, but he used to find it difficult. He can understand simple emotions, like when someone is feeling happy or sad. So he knows that a smile means someone is happy. Sometimes if I pretend to cry, he'll come over and shake me to try and stop me from crying. 'Don't be sad, Mummy,' he says.

Harvey likes a strict, daily routine and he can get upset if things change. But because of my lifestyle and my job, that can be hard. I don't have a set daily routine. It's not like I wake up and go to work 9-5, my schedule differs.

I try to keep it as calm as possible, but sometimes I can be called somewhere and I have to leave as soon as possible. With the other children, I can be like, 'Come on kids, get in the car!' But with Harvey, it's much slower. It can be an absolute nightmare getting him in the car. Sometimes I have to really persuade him. I'll say something like, 'Get in the car and we can stop off at the station and get you a cheese sandwich.' And that usually gets him moving!

Another key sign of autism is having a very keen interest in certain subjects. That's definitely true in Harvey's case. I think you know by now it's trains, frogs and his bloody iPad.

People with autism can also find it hard to make friends or prefer to be on their own. Harvey definitely likes his own company, but he can make friends. I guess the term 'friends' is different for Harvey, though.

With my friends, I tell them everything and we go for dinner together and go shopping, whereas I suppose Harvey having a friend is just him being able to sit there and communicate with someone. Even if it's just asking a question like, 'Do you like that train?' or, 'Do you like my drawing?'

With his family, it's a different kind of relationship. I guess he can have a much deeper connection with us because he's known us all his life.

Attention deficit hyperactivity disorder (ADHD)
Along with autism, Harvey also has ADHD. It means that he has a short attention span and is easily distracted. Sometimes he's unable to stick to tasks that are time-consuming, and he can find it difficult to understand instructions.

If I tell him to do something, he might struggle to know what I mean and then he gets frustrated. So I have to speak to him in a clear voice.

Harvey also has no sense of danger, which is common with ADHD, and that's why someone always has to be with him.

Oppositional defiant disorder (ODD)
This is another condition I find hard to deal with as it's all about behaviour.

It causes temper tantrums and sudden rages, which can be triggered by the smallest of incidents. Which is exactly what Harvey is like.

He can also be very stubborn. For example, if I wanted him to wear a certain pair of shoes to match his outfit and he didn't want to wear them, he wouldn't.

Instead, he prefers to wear a pair of shoes that are on their last legs and ready to be put in the bin! He has so many scruffy old shoes that he won't let me throw away because he loves them so much.

Prader-Willi syndrome

We got this diagnosis a bit later in Harvey's life, shortly after he became a teenager. It's a genetic condition, but it's very rare to have more than one child with Prader-Willi syndrome.

When someone has Prader-Willi syndrome, everything revolves around food because they always want to eat. Food is constantly on Harvey's mind.

If I leave Harvey in a room on his own, he'll check through all the cupboards looking for food. Sometimes I can tell he's been in the cupboards because I find him with crumbs all around his mouth. I'll be like, 'Harv, what have you just eaten?' And he says, 'Nothing, Mummy.' I say, 'Are you sure? What about the crumbs around your mouth?' And then he starts kicking off because I've caught him out.

I've had people in the house before and he will go through their bags to see if they've got sweets or anything for him to eat. You have to really watch him!

If I've told him he can't have any more food, he'll wait until I'm gone and say to someone else, 'I'm hungry!' He knows how to manipulate a situation to get food from someone. And he always remembers people who have given him food in the past.

He even goes through the bins sometimes and he's been known to eat frozen food from the freezer. He doesn't care if it tastes horrible because to him, food is food.

In the past, he has gotten up in the night and raided the fridge without me knowing. I've woken up in the morning and realised what he's taken out of the fridge. He can just eat and eat and eat, which is very worrying when it comes to his weight gain. It got to the point where I had to stop buying treats full stop, because Harvey would just sneakily eat them all. But then it wasn't fair on the other children.

It's also quite common that adults with Prader-Willi syndrome steal money so that they can get food. But Harvey doesn't steal money because he doesn't understand the concept of it. He doesn't know that money buys food.

If he doesn't get food, he'll start kicking off and having a tantrum until he gets what he wants. It can be quite hard to not give in to him, but I have to think of his health.

He also loves taking pictures of his food. If we're having a meal, he'll take lots of close-ups on his iPad. He takes about 100 pictures and it's the same picture over and over again. But that's not just with food, that's with everything!

Most children with Prader-Willi syndrome have difficult behavioural problems. It can cause controlling and manipulative behaviour. Harvey definitely isn't malicious in any way, but he can be manipulative. Especially when food is involved.

Prader-Willi syndrome also causes poor sexual development. Harvey has no desire for a romantic relationship. He has had girlfriends in the past, but it's not like a proper relationship. He had his first girlfriend when he was 14 and he was with her for two years. For his birthday, she bought him some aftershave. It was very innocent and sweet, where they just held hands – it was more like a friendship.

Harvey has never spoken about sex. I don't think he would have a clue what it is. He's so childlike, I can't ever imagine him speaking about sex. I've never seen him experiment or have a fiddle down there like most teenage boys – and I'm glad I haven't. I know that a lot of young adults with disabilities do, and they have to be taught to do it in private.

When I spoke to the teachers at Harvey's school, I told them that Harvey doesn't do anything like that. They told me they get cases where students have sometimes done it in the classroom.

Underactive thyroid (hypothyroidism)

This condition is the main reason for Harvey's weight gain because he doesn't have the hormones to regulate his metabolism. He takes tablets to treat it, but he's still very big. It also causes him to get tired very easily. He sleeps a lot and he's usually tucked up in bed at around 7pm every night.

Anxiety and depression

Harvey suffers very badly with anxiety. It's normally when he's not with me or if he's out of his comfort zone – he can get quite distressed. He's also been diagnosed with depression. Depression affects everyone in a different way. It's not like Harvey feels suicidal, but he does have episodes where he goes through extreme sadness.

Tic disorder

Harvey has a few different tics. He twitches his body all the time, he rocks his body and he also slaps his belly. For Harvey, they're usually associated with excitement or happiness.

Self-harming behaviour (picking of the skin)

Harvey has had this for years. I guess there's different aspects to self-harming. Some people self-harm because they don't want to be here any more. But Harvey's self-harm is more for his sensory needs.

He enjoys the feeling of picking his skin and he likes to look at the shape it makes on his body. And then once he makes himself bleed, he likes the feeling of touching the blood and wiping it on the wall. He does it all over his body. He has scabs on his arms and legs and they've become scarred. It looks like he's covered in mosquito bites.

Sometimes he picks the scar from the burn on his leg and we've had to go to the hospital a few times because it gets infected. That's why I have to make sure his nails are short and clean.

Harvey can also take things very literally. So, to get him to stop, I say to him, 'If you keep picking your leg, your leg is going to fall off and you'll have to hop.' And then he becomes scared and says, 'No, Mum!'

He doesn't seem to feel the same pain as us. Harvey can bang his head against the wall repeatedly and smash holes in furniture with his fists, but he doesn't get hurt. We were once on holiday and we went into a restaurant which had a huge glass cabinet fish tank. And what did he do? He headbutted it and it cracked. I was so embarrassed! The glass they use for those fish tanks is extremely thick, so that just shows how strong he is.

Obesity

This one is pretty self-explanatory. Harvey is obese. It's complicated because his Prader-Willi syndrome makes him want to eat a lot, but we have that under control and we make sure he's not overeating. As I said, his weight gain is because of his underactive thyroid. Harvey will always have challenging behaviour and he'll always be on medication, and that will never change. He has to be closely monitored, but the doctors are really worried about his weight because it could cause a heart attack.

We're trying really hard to help him lose weight. I mean, he's never going to be slim with a six-pack. Although I would love to see him like that. It's just Harvey's belly we need to try to get rid of – it's absolutely huge. And he has a habit of lifting up his T-shirt and showing it off. Sometimes I wish I could just get a pair of scissors and cut it off. We're doing our best to encourage him to exercise, and I'm hoping that he'll become more active at college.

Seventeen

MEDICATION

I always joke that Harvey takes so many tablets that he rattles when he walks. Without his medication, he would die. It's as simple as that.

His medication box goes everywhere with him and it's huge. Half of the tablets keep him alive, and the other half are to help with his behavioural issues. He is so challenging – and that's with the help of medication. So I can't even imagine what he'd be like without it.

He doesn't like taking his medication, but he's very good at it. I tell him to open his mouth wide and he takes all the tablets in one go. I don't know how he does it – it makes me gag just watching him.

He has set times he needs to take them – and I'm

basically his human alarm clock. He's been on medication all of his life, so my brain is just programmed to know when it's time for his tablets. He's currently on 11 different types of medication which he has to take at set times throughout the day.

The only complication is that taking all of his medications together can be dangerous. It's like taking a cocktail of drugs, so the doctors have to be really sure they have the right balance.

Harvey has to go for a lot of tests to see if they need to make any changes to his prescriptions. He has a blood test every six months and they also take a urine sample. Sometimes you can give too much of some tablets and too little of others, so he has to be assessed and they're always getting adjusted.

As Harvey gets older and bigger, it's constantly changing. Some of the doses seem quite small and you wonder how it could have any affect on someone Harvey's size. But it just goes to show that you shouldn't underestimate a tablet. We have to be very strict – Harvey can't take any more than what is advised.

The tablets for his physical health are prescribed by Great Ormond Street, and the ones for his behaviour and mental health are from Maudsley. He visits each hospital separately, but they communicate with each other about the medication. I speak to the doctors every two to three weeks to give them updates on Harvey. They're so good. I can't praise them enough.

Because he takes so many tablets on a daily basis, we run out of them by the end of the week. So I have to pick up his prescriptions weekly. You really have to keep on top of it and be on the ball because they don't just come in automatically, you have to keep reordering them.

Desmopressin was the first medication Harvey started taking and it was for his diabetes insipidus. This controls the waterworks in his body, and if he doesn't take it, it can be very dangerous. His body would shut down and he would die. When he first started taking it, I used to give him it mixed with water in a syringe, but now he's older he can take it in tablet form.

Out of all the tablets Harvey takes, there's one in particular that he *really* hates. It's purple and he takes it for his ADHD. Harvey always says, 'No. Not the purple one.' If he sees it, he goes mad. I'm not sure why he dislikes it so much as he takes much bigger tablets than this one. It must have a funny taste to it. I have to try to turn it into a game and pretend I'm throwing it away before it goes in his mouth, otherwise it can be a nightmare trying to force him to have it.

I also have to inject a growth hormone into Harvey every day. While he was going through puberty, the dosage had to be higher because he needed a bit of a kick start. People find it confusing because he's so big, so they question why he needs it, but it's because his body can't produce the normal amount of hormones. I used to absolutely hate giving him it. I'd have to wake up in the middle of the night to inject him – and as you know, I hate needles. But I've been doing it for years, so I'm just used to it now.

I know that Harvey will be on medication for the rest of his life but, like I said, he's needed it since he was a baby so he doesn't know any different. I can't thank the NHS and all the doctors enough for helping us when it comes to keeping Harvey as happy and healthy as he possibly can be.

Eighteen

SUITED AND BOOTED

'We're going to the NTAs. Do you know how cool that is?' I kept asking Harvey in the car as we made our way to The O2, in London, on Thursday 9 September 2021.

I'd been explaining to him for months that he was up for an award because people loved watching his programme, *Harvey And Me*, on the TV. But I don't think he realised just how much of a big deal it was.

It wasn't my first time attending the NTAs, but it was my first time attending as a nominee for my own show. But it wasn't about winning. The fact *Harvey And Me* was even nominated for Authored Documentary in the first place was an amazing achievement. And then to find out that we'd been shortlisted was incredible. We already felt like winners.

Harvey came back from college especially for the occasion. There was no way I was going to let him miss it. He was so excited to see me and I was so excited to see him. He'd only been at college for two weeks at this point, but I was so happy to have my baby boy back in my arms.

We spent the whole day getting ready in a hotel – and I made sure that we both dressed to impress. It's a once-in-a-lifetime opportunity, so I wanted to go all out for it.

I wanted Harvey to look dapper, but it's so hard to find smart clothes for him because of his size. I was going to get something tailor-made, until Ben from Uptheir clothing – who Harvey has his range with – got in touch.

He asked me if he could help organise an outfit for Harvey, and he very kindly sent some black trousers and a black shirt for him to wear. As Ben is autistic, he can be quite regimented. So he actually sent me 20 black shirts and 20 pairs of trousers, just in case he had got the wrong size. Bless him! He knew Harvey's size, but he sent lots of different ones just to be sure – which was so thoughtful.

I bought Harvey some black and gold Versace trainers – real Verace may I add – and a big Versace medallion. I really did go all out! I just thought, 'Why the hell not?' It was his big night and he deserved it.

To help with the noise of the event, I also got him some crystalised ear defenders with a green 'H' in the middle. The woman who made them had made me some crystalised crutches when I broke my feet last year. She'd done such a good job, so I knew Harvey would love them.

He also got his hair done for the night. He went for a skin fade with two razor lines and he got his beard trimmed, too. He looked so grown up! He was fully kitted and ready to go. I shared a picture of him on our family WhatsApp group chat and my mum was like, 'He can't go dressed like that! He looks like Mr. T!' I was like, 'It's called fashion, Mum!'

I wanted to match with Harvey, so I wore a black and gold Versace shirt. But I had a bit of a wardrobe malfunction as soon as we were about to leave. I noticed there was a button missing on the cuff of the shirt and it was really obvious.

I wouldn't usually care, but I knew that it would look obvious in the photos that would be taken of us. Plus, I'd paid quite a lot of money for it! I ended up covering it up with some Versace bracelets, but if you look at the pictures from the night you can clearly see there's a button missing.

I paired it with some black flares and some Versace crystal heels. And no, I'm not sponsored by Versace! It was the first time I had risked wearing six-inch heels since breaking my feet. I wore them because I knew I could hold on to Harvey for support when we walked the red carpet, but I was in agony.

My sister also came along for the occasion. I got my hair and make-up done, but Sophie chose to do her own. She always looks so natural and gorgeous. She was taking the piss out of me and my Versace outfit. She was laughing, saying, 'It's a far cry from my ASOS outfit and £20 shoes!' But Sophie could wear a bin bag and still look good.

I went for something a bit different with my hair. You know me, I'm not afraid to try out a bold look. I mean, we've all seen my outfits from some of my book launches in the past! I wore my hair up with a huge plait that almost touched the floor. Apparently, the singer Ashanti had the exact same hairstyle at the MTV VMAs a couple of days later. Just putting it out there, I did it first!

It was my first red carpet in about two years, and it was Harvey's first proper one. He went to Disney premieres and things like that when he was younger, but nothing on this scale. I'm not going to lie, I was absolutely shitting myself.

I'm always nervous about doing red carpets anyway. I've done a lot in my time, but it never gets any easier. I get so worked up in the car on the way, and then I make everyone around me nervous. So many thoughts run through my head.

'Do I need a wee? Am I going to get booed? What if I trip up?'

But as soon as I get out there, I go into full work mode. It's really nerve-racking because you know you're going to be looked at from every single angle. I'm constantly telling myself, 'Breathe in, hold the bag, smile and wave.' A lot more goes into it than just walking down a carpet.

The experience of the red carpet at the NTAs was very different this year. It wasn't as busy as what it has been in the past. There were no members of the public behind the railings and there weren't as many journalists – it actually felt a bit like a ghost town.

I had no idea how Harvey was going to react. He didn't kick off, which is the main thing. I kept telling him how well he was doing and that when we got home, he could have some carrot cake.

We did all the press interviews on the red carpet together, but I could see that Harvey was getting tired and agitated, so I made sure we weren't hanging around for too long. He was getting bored of just standing around and his legs were becoming restless.

Journalists were asking him questions and he just kept yawning. He's usually asleep by 7pm, so it was a late night for him. I had to repeat the questions they were asking so that he could answer them. I think people only realise when they meet him that he can actually be quite difficult to talk to. After our interviews, it was time for us to get our pictures taken. People were pulling us in all different directions. It was Sophie's first experience of a red carpet, so I think it was a bit of a shock to the system for her.

You'd think it would be straightforward, just walking along and having your picture taken, but it's quite stressful. Especially with Harvey. But he was really up for having some pictures taken. I was saying, 'Smile, Harv!' and he was opening his mouth wide. We also took some pictures of the three of us together, and then they wanted some single shots of me. They're photos I can look back on fondly and treasure the memories of such a special night.

As soon as we walked inside, everyone was looking at Harvey and he got a lot of attention. I think people are just fascinated by him. Some people in the crowd were calling out his name, so he got up and started waving at them – it was so cute. He loved it.

I think his favourite part of the night was when JLS performed. He got up and started dancing to all their songs. He really got into it and I could tell he was enjoying himself.

It was quite a long wait until it got to our category, and I could see that Harvey was getting tired. But as soon as he saw himself on the big screen he stood up and started clapping. He was so excited.

We were up against the likes of Kate Garraway, Rob Burrow, Roman Kemp and Marcus Rashford – four amazing people. Everyone kept telling me they thought we were going to win, but I wasn't expecting to. I know everyone says it, but I really wasn't.

Davina McCall was presenting the award and I was so nervous when she opened the envelope. I hadn't prepared a speech, so if we had won, I have no idea what I would have said. And God only knows what would have come out of Harvey's mouth!

When Davina announced *Kate Garraway: Finding Derek* as the winner, I was really happy for Kate. Harvey got up and started clapping for her – he was very gracious about it!

If I'm honest, I think we all deserved to win. But obviously there can only be one winner. When you look at all five of the documentaries, we've all had such different and compelling stories. They're hard to compare because they're all brilliant in their own way. Kate thoroughly deserved it, though.

To be fair, she's on breakfast TV every day, so she had a good platform to promote her documentary as she could reach a lot of people. That isn't a dig by the way and that's not me being bitter, it's just the way it is.

I really like Kate. I actually had a really good conversation with her. I spoke about what it's like being a carer for Harvey, and she spoke about how she's now a carer for her husband Derek. It just goes to show that anything can happen in life and anyone can become a carer for a loved one, so you shouldn't judge – and yes Frankie Boyle, that's aimed at you. And to all the other trolls out there.

The ceremony began at 7.30pm and you had to stay seated right up until it finished at 10pm. They did ask if Harvey wanted to be seated in a different room, but I said no. I know they mean well and I appreciate it, but the point I always try to make is that I want Harvey to be treated like everyone else. I don't want him to be isolated.

Considering there was a lot of noise, lights and music, he did really well. He sat through the whole thing and I was really proud of him. He wanted to go home as soon as it ended, so there was no mingling in the bar area for Harvey. He chose his bed over a glass of orange squash. And I don't blame him!

His carer came along with us for the evening and she took him back to the hotel while I stayed out for a little bit longer to catch up with people I hadn't seen for ages. It was really nice to see some familiar faces. The last time I saw some of them was just before I went into The Priory, so I wasn't in my best head space at the time. I now feel the best I've ever felt and my mindset is so clear.

It was such a lovely night. It wasn't about me, it was all

about Harvey. It was his night. But unfortunately, a huge dampener was put on the evening because I made the headlines the next day for all the wrong reasons. I really don't know why. The whole place was full of celebrities, and who makes the front page of *The Sun*? Me. That's who!

I can't believe I even have to justify myself, but the reports couldn't have been further from the truth. I was there with Harvey all night long before he left to go to bed. I stayed with the producer of our documentary, Hannah Lowes, and the rest of the team just to show my face for a bit. I was there for an extra 45 minutes and in that time, according to the press, I was over every man in the room.

Apparently I was also on a massive booze bender. Yes, I had a little drink. So what? So did everyone else! It certainly wasn't a 'booze bender'. It was a social event. There was a bottle of champagne at the end of each row and they were filling up our glasses during the ad breaks.

Ruth Langsford and Eamonn Holmes, who are absolute legends by the way, had a big bottle of Moët next to them – were they criticised for that? No they weren't. I wanted to celebrate and enjoy some champagne. I knew I wasn't going to over step the mark and let myself down because I know my limits. It's not like I was going round stumbling all over and causing a scene. It's a shame I even have to go there, but I hope that's cleared everything up.

I don't know why the press enjoys picking on me so much. I don't care if you like me or dislike me, but I feel like people get a buzz out of putting a downer on everything I do.

I was there to celebrate an amazing achievement with my son, yet they still put me on the front page to try and bring me down. It just ruins it and makes me question why I even bother going to an event. If we'd have won the award, I doubt they'd have put that on their front pages. They never focus on the positive. Anyway, I'm not going to let that overshadow Harvey's success. I just wanted to get it off my chest.

How many 19-year-olds can say they've been nominated for an award? We may not have won, but Harvey will always be a winner in my eyes. Besides, there's always next year for documentary number two. So bring it on, I say!

Nineteen

THE NEXT CHAPTER

Friday 27 August 2021. The day I'd been dreading for months – the day it was time to finally let go of my baby boy. He's definitely not a baby any more and he hates it when I call him that, but he always will be to me.

As I've been writing this book, it's made me realise just how much Harvey and I have been through. It's funny because I never really think about it. I just get on with it. But when you're forced to sit down and go through past memories, it makes you look back on just how far you've come.

I was told Harvey didn't have much of a chance in life, so never in a million years did I think he'd be starting college. But then again, I've never given up hope. I'm bursting with pride, but it's also been really hard for me to accept.

Harvey has been with me throughout everything. Yes, he's been at his residential school for the past couple of years, but I'd see him every weekend and he was only an hour away. This is different.

I don't like the thought of being apart from him. I've always felt secure knowing that no one can take Harvey away from me, and I know it sounds stupid, but this feels like he's being taken away from me.

He has to have his own identity now. He can't always have his mum there. You of course want your son to be in your family unit, but you also have to do what's best for him.

Sometimes I find myself speaking for Harvey. When people ask him questions, I answer them for him. I don't mean to do it, it's just what I've become used to. Harvey hasn't always been able to have a voice, but now it's time for him to find that voice.

I've got to let Harvey have the best shot at life. And to do that, I have to let him go. Don't get me wrong, I'm not just taking him off to college and never seeing him again. But it will be a big change for the both of us.

I'd been preparing myself for the day for a while, but I don't think I could ever have been fully prepared for Harvey to officially fly the nest.

He actually woke up in a really good mood in the morning. 'You're going to college, Harv. Are you excited?' I kept asking him. 'Yes, Mum,' he said, as he rocked his body back and forth. That's when you know he's excited. From the day he got accepted, I kept explaining to him that he was going to college and becoming a man. Because of his anxiety, I wanted to make sure he was really prepared for it so that he wasn't scared or confused.

I'd say to him, 'When you go to college, you're going to be a proper adult. You're going to have your own bedroom, your own bathroom and your own kitchen. And you can meet new friends.' He'd reply, 'Oh yay, Mum,' in an excited voice. And then I'd ask him how he felt, and he'd say, 'Happy, Mummy,' and give me a big thumbs up. It was nice to know he was looking forward to it.

So, I packed the car full of Harvey's belongings and off we went to the National Star College in Cheltenham, where he'll be staying full-time until he's 25.

But let me rewind a little bit first and explain how we got here. Finding a college for Harvey wasn't easy. If you watched *Harvey And Me*, you'll have seen how difficult it was to find somewhere that felt right for the both of us.

I always knew it would be a challenge trying to find a college that could cater to his needs, but 'challenge' is an understatement.

When you're looking for colleges, your local authority

sends you a list – and they could be anywhere in the country. I was sent a list of about 40 different colleges and they were in places like Sunderland, Yorkshire and Leicestershire. Miles away from us, basically! So I ruled those out straight away.

Harvey needed to be living on-site, so it's not like he'd have to travel there in a car every day, but I just didn't like the thought of him being so far away from home. From the list, there were only three local ones, and I had it in my head that it would have to be one of the three because there was no way I was letting him go somewhere far away.

I visited them with Harvey, but I just couldn't picture him at any of them. And I knew that he didn't like them either. They just didn't feel right – you get a gut feeling. Harvey is going to be staying at college for six years, so it had to be somewhere that we were comfortable with.

Even when I was looking at schools for Harvey when he was younger, there were certain things I was looking out for. I like to look around a school or college and see colourful walls. I want to know that Harvey is going to be stimulated. I'd never put him in some hospital-feeling, sterile environment.

I wouldn't take my baby to a nursery with just white, plain walls and all the toys tidied away. You want to see toys everywhere, with things stuck to the walls like drawings, the letters of the alphabet, numbers and animals. So it shouldn't be different with colleges.

I think it's also good to see how the staff react when children are misbehaving. It's a good insight into how they deal with a difficult child. In some places, there'd be a child kicking off and the teacher would just close the door and send us to the next room. That was a major red flag to me. I'd much rather see how they handle it so that I know how they'd cope with Harvey.

Because I knew he would be living at the college, their living spaces were another big thing to consider. I didn't like the look of some of the rooms. I wanted it to feel homely, whereas some of them were really bland and looked more like prisons.

A couple of the colleges also had constant banging doors throughout the building, which obviously was an instant no as Harvey wouldn't last two minutes there without smashing the place up.

There was one college in particular where Harvey started kicking off because a door slammed as soon as we arrived – even though I had warned them that Harvey hates doors banging. I was in my wheelchair at the time as well because of my broken feet, so it was a nightmare trying to calm him down.

Harvey was going absolutely mad and I could see some of the staff members looking at him with a worried expression, probably thinking, 'How could we cope with him?' I know that not every college is going to cater to Harvey's hatred of doors banging, but I'd seen that a lot of them had silent closing doors or automatic doors, so I knew I wasn't being unreasonable.

After a string of unsuccessful viewings, I had to be a bit more open-minded about my choices. But actually, it was very slim pickings. Each college has a list of needs that they can cater for, which sounds quite brutal, but it's just a fact that they can't cater to every disabled young adult because not everywhere has the facilities.

I was surprised by this, but the two things that made it hard to find a college for Harvey were the fact he's visually impaired and that he has Prader-Willi syndrome. I presumed that being visually impaired would be one of the more common conditions, but apparently not. So, that narrowed it down to just five colleges in the end – including National Star. When I first saw that it was in Cheltenham, I said, 'Absolutely no way. Not a chance!' I ruled it out instantly. It's about a four-hour drive away from us, which is way too far.

But the more I researched National Star, the more it appealed to me. It sounded amazing for Harvey. I still wasn't sold on the idea of him moving miles away, but I wanted us to go and have a look around. When we first visited, Harvey kicked off straight away. We hadn't even walked through the front doors yet and he was already causing havoc.

'Oh no, is this a bad omen?' I thought to myself. I had to use my usual techniques to get him out of the car and calm him down. We'd come all this way, so we were staying here whether Harvey liked it or not.

Once he was inside and the staff started showing us around, Harvey absolutely loved it – and I loved it. Like I said before, you just get that gut feeling.

It was in the countryside and it had lovely surroundings – there was lots of greenery. The views from the bedrooms were so picturesque. It had a swimming pool, a gym, a music room and an arts and crafts room. It even had a radio station that the students could work at.

There was also a huge sensory room with bubble tubes, which are his favourite, and a projector where he could watch videos of trains, roller-coasters and frogs. The staff were so good with Harvey. I could totally imagine him living there. It was perfect. There was just one small problem… the fact it was in Cheltenham. I just couldn't get my head around it being so far away.

But in the end, I had to. I didn't have a choice. National Star ticked every single box and I had to keep telling myself that if I wanted a good college, it wouldn't be on our doorstep.

So, the next step was putting in an application for

Harvey. The local authority funds his place at the college, so they have to agree to it first.

The college sends them a funding application, which details everything they provide to Harvey and how much it will cost. Full-time residential alongside his healthcare needs costs the Government around £350,000 per year.

I don't need to justify anything, but I guess some people might question why I wouldn't pay for the college myself if I can afford it. Especially after the whole debate about me not paying for Harvey's school driver. But it's nothing to do with me, it's for Harvey. He's 19 and he's an adult and those are his rights. You wouldn't expect a mum with an able 19-year-old to pay for their house and pay all of their bills for them. They go out to work and earn their own money. So why should it be different?

The application process was a real struggle. For one, all the forms are online and I'm terrible at technology. But thankfully, you do get help with it. There's no way I could have done it on my own.

The thing is, a lot of people think that Harvey is more able than what he actually is. Yes, he is able to do a lot of things, but his behaviour does affect him. And although he functions and he can talk, he has a lot of medical needs. He doesn't understand danger and because he's visually impaired, he does need 24-hour care.

The local authority questioned why Harvey couldn't

live at home and travel to a college, rather than live on site. I explained that we'd tried before during his school years at Linden Lodge and it just didn't work. He'd kick off every single day and refuse to go to school. But the local authority really tried to argue it.

To me, there is no argument. There's no way Harvey could travel in the car every day because he ends up kicking off and smashing windows, and he's a danger to himself and everyone around him. If they saw it for themselves, they'd understand.

In the end, we had to get Harvey's doctors involved because they've known him his whole life and know the true extent of how challenging he really is.

We provided lots of documents to the local authority to prove that he needed to be there full-time, and then we just had to wait for their decision. There were two people on the board making the decision. I felt like one of them was in support of Harvey going to National Star, but it seemed like the other was trying to find every reason why he shouldn't. There was a very big question mark over whether they would accept Harvey's application. I had no idea what would happen. It was totally 50/50.

It was a stressful time and I found it very draining. I kept thinking, 'If he doesn't get accepted, what the hell are we going to do now?' If you're going through a similar process, my advice to anyone is to give yourself at least a year in advance to prepare and organise everything. I just presumed it would be easy, but it took a very long time. I usually am very lastminute.com with everything, but with this, you definitely can't afford to be. You have to be patient, but it's totally worth it.

A few weeks went by and I finally received the phone call from the local authority. 'We're pleased to let you know that your application has been accepted.'

My first thought was, 'Brilliant!' It was such a relief and I was over the moon. But my next thought was, 'Shit!' It suddenly all felt very real.

I'd kind of just put it to the back of my mind because I didn't want to imagine being without Harvey. I kept telling myself, 'Just don't think about it, Katie.' I just couldn't get the thought out of my head that Harvey was going to be taken away from me until he was 25. But I had to keep reminding myself that wasn't the case at all. He's just going to college and it's good for him.

So, back to Friday 27 August. I'd been dreading the car journey. I hated the thought of dropping Harvey off and driving home without him by my side. But like I said, Harvey was so excited, which made me feel so much better. If he was upset and kicking off, I just don't know how I would have coped. On the way there, I was just constantly cuddling and kissing him and telling him how much I loved him.

As soon as we got there, he wanted to get out of the car and go straight to his room. He was walking miles ahead of me – he couldn't get there quick enough!

'Mum, look at my room!' he said, and he started showing me everything. His room is perfect for him. He's got such a big area. It's like having his own little studio flat. It's basically a bachelor pad, but without the parties – I hope!

He's got a big bed, a TV which is built into a cabinet so that he can't smash it, a massive walk-in wet room with a shower, and a kitchen area. In the kitchen, he's got a washing machine, a hob, a toaster and a kettle. I can't wait for him to learn some more life skills and just become independent.

He's already learnt how to put the washing machine on, which is amazing. They make it easier for them to use, so it's just one button to press.

At home, he used to help unload the dishwasher and he'd help me in the kitchen. He's done a bit of cooking in the past, but he has to have someone with him. For example, he's helped me make a cake before. He cracked the eggs himself and mixed it all up. He's also made cheese sandwiches for us all. He never fails to impress me. His favourite meal is spaghetti carbonara, so maybe he'll be able to make that from scratch one day. He may even follow in his mum's footsteps and appear on *MasterChef*!

But my challenge for him at the moment is for him to be able to make me a cup of tea. As he's partially sighted, it can be quite dangerous for him with the boiling water. But you can buy a device that you put in a cup which makes a beeping noise when you've got the water high enough, so that you don't burn yourself. So I'm going to get him one of them to help him.

I just want him to learn and better himself. Even little things, like learning how to shower himself. He can get in the shower and rinse himself, but I want him to learn how to do it properly. He can get himself dressed, but I want him to learn to get his clothes out of the washing machine, fold them up and put them away. I want him to be able to make his bed and tidy his room. It's just the things we take for granted, but that Harvey finds difficult.

His room is decorated really nicely. He's got a light wooden floor and they've painted the walls green especially for him. Everything I've bought for him is green – even the dustpan and brush. He's also got a green blanket with frog bedding, of course. I still need to take some other bits to him, like his computer and piano. But he's got the basics for now.

My only worry is that he'll smash his room up. He has three big windows that open up and as soon as I saw them, I said to the staff, 'Bloody hell, you're brave putting

Harvey in a room like this.' We will see how long those windows stay like that! Once we've got all the furniture in his room and he's properly settled in, they're going to bolt everything to the floor so that he can't pick anything up and throw it.

The journey back home wasn't as bad as I expected. I didn't make a big fuss of saying bye to him. I gave him a big cuddle and a kiss and told him I would see him soon.

Even though we'd unpacked and he was all settled in, I still don't think it had really sunk in at that point. It took me five hours to get home because the traffic was so bad, so to be honest, that didn't make me feel great. It only reiterated how far away he was. I had Jett and Bunny in the car with me as they came along for the journey, so they certainly kept me entertained and kept my mind off it.

I'm slowly starting to get over the distance now. I've been reminding myself that he's absolutely fine. In fact, he's more than fine – he's loving it! He's got a lovely room and it's his home away from home. I know he's settled in and enjoying himself. But I'm not going to lie, I feel totally lost without him.

I've been responsible for him all his life, so now it feels weird to have this freedom. I look at the clock and I'm like, 'It's 2pm, I need to give him his medication.' And then I think, 'Oh, Harvey isn't here.' It's a strange feeling and it's going to take some getting used to.

The college constantly gives me updates on how he's doing, which is nice. Whoever is looking after him on the day sends me pictures of Harvey and tells me what he's up to. Apparently he keeps asking to go for a 'healthy walk' around the grounds. He calls it a healthy walk because his doctors always encourage him to go for walks to help with this weight. So that's reassuring to hear!

I still FaceTime him every day, too. And every time I've spoken to him, he says it's fantastic. When he says that, I know he really does love it. He's been telling me all about the work he's been doing, like maths and English. They've even got their own shop on-site, which is good for teaching the students how to handle money. So I've been giving him some money so that he can go there to buy something and pay for it himself.

He hasn't really had to do that before. In the past, if I've given him pocket money, I ask him what he wants to spend it on and he'll say, 'Muffins and cake.' He doesn't really have a concept of money.

They take them out to shops away from the college as well, so he'll be out of his comfort zone. It really is the next step into adulthood for Harvey. As I mentioned, they have their own radio station, so I'm hoping he'll get involved and have a small segment on there. I think he'd be great at that, although they may need to put a warning for strong adult language before he goes on air!

So far, he's had one wobbly moment where he said, 'Mummy, I need you and I miss you.' But that's completely normal for him. The only other time he's been a bit funny is when it comes to brushing his teeth or having a shower – he's like a typical teenager. He usually gets showered twice a day, but he's not so keen on a shower in the evening because he gets tired, so that's when he kicks off. But I'm sure the staff there will soon learn his ways.

Harvey will be living at National Star for 52 weeks of the year, which means he can stay there as long as he likes – even throughout all of the holidays, including Christmas. Obviously he's going to come home, but it's a relief to know that he can always be there. It's a real security blanket for me.

For example, if something dramatic happened in my life, and let's be honest, that's a common occurrence, I don't have to be thinking, 'What's going to happen to Harvey? Who's going to look after him?' It's a massive weight off my shoulders to know that if he absolutely has to, he can stay there. I feel like now, for the first time, I can breathe. And even though I do, I shouldn't feel guilty for that.

Every weekend, it used to be like, 'Right, I've got all the kids. What are we going to do?' And there were certain things I couldn't do because I'd have Harvey, and I'd hate having to leave him.

But now, he can spend the weekend at college with the students. There are lots of young adults who he'll be able to have some banter and a joke with. I've been told there are lots of cheeky characters there like Harvey, so I'm sure he'll make lots of friends. And I can't wait to meet them. Harvey is one of the youngest at the college, so I'm sure he'll be able to learn a lot from some of the older students who have already been there a couple of years.

They go out in groups and they're taken to places like the cinema or bowling. They've even got a student bar. Not that Harvey will be drinking! I can't even imagine what would happen to Harvey if he had alcohol. They advise you not to drink on tablets, so God knows how that would end. But luckily, I know he's never going to try it because he doesn't like it. He'll stick to his water or orange squash.

I'm sure he'll love the bar, though. Harvey really wants to go to a nightclub. He keeps telling me he wants to go to one and do a backflip on the dancefloor. Not that he can do a backflip, but he thinks he can.

Harvey is used to seeing me every weekend and he can come home whenever he wants, but I've explained to him that some weekends he might not even want to see me. He might want to go bowling or go to the cinema with his friends. That's what I'm hoping for. It's selfish for me to have him at home with me all the time. He needs to explore the bigger world and he has every right to explore it.

I can visit Harvey whenever I want, which is reassuring to know. I just have to let the college know in advance. I'm already so excited about visiting him. I'm going to make a real effort to go there rather than bringing him home because it would be a long journey for him.

I don't think it's fair on him to have a full day at college, get into a car during Friday night traffic and then spend most of Sunday travelling. It'd mean he'd only have the Saturday at home – and he'd be so tired he'd probably spend it sleeping anyway.

Now that he's there, I can imagine it could be so easy to say, 'I don't need to see him.' And I don't want that to ever happen. I can't stand the thought of Harvey sitting there and wondering why he isn't seeing me as often. Even if I'm busy, I've promised myself I will make the time to travel to see him no matter what.

It's difficult at the minute because I don't have my driving licence. I can't wait to be able to drive again. It's really started to affect me, especially now that Harvey is four hours away. I've always been independent and not being able to drive when it's what you're used to is really difficult.

My house in Horsham is in the middle of nowhere and I can't even walk to a shop. I have to find a driver or find someone to drive me. So it's very draining to know that Harvey is hours away and I can't get in a car. I'm counting down the days until I can drive again.

The other struggle is the fact he's so far away from the family. It's hard enough trying to organise a family get-together somewhere local, never mind getting them all in a car to Cheltenham to see Harvey.

I think my mum will find it particularly hard, but she knows it's good for him. The kids are getting older and they have their own lives, but I want to make sure they're still making the effort to see their brother.

In Harvey's world, his family are his absolute everything. Every time he draws pictures, he'll include us all. For example, he draws a family of frogs and he names us all. He draws a mummy frog and her baby frogs, Harvey, Junior, Princess, Jett and Bunny.

Junior and Princess are growing up and doing their own things, but to Harvey, he doesn't know what's going on in the big wide world. He's in his own little bubble. Jett and Bunny are already missing him. They keep asking me when we can visit him at his new home. Because they were with me when we dropped him off, I think leaving him there has made it more real for them.

Moving to college and becoming a man also means he will no longer be under the care of Great Ormond Street. Once you turn 18, you're an adult in the eyes of the law.

Harvey is currently transitioning from children's health care to adult's health care, which can take a while.

I've lived and breathed that hospital all of his life, so it's such a weird feeling. They know everything about him – they know how he behaves and what medication he needs.

A big worry for me is that if he has to go into hospital, he'll be going somewhere unfamiliar and it'll all be very different to what he's used to. I also fear they won't be able to cope with him. But I guess he can't stay at Great Ormond Street forever.

Another thing that worried me about Harvey moving away was the fact I wouldn't be there to protect him. While filming *Harvey And Me*, I'd read stories about people like Harvey getting sectioned under the Mental Health Act.

I didn't even know that it was a thing, but it's very real. It really did terrify me. I met up with a woman called Isabelle Garnett, whose son Matthew was sectioned when he was 15 for 15 months.

Like Harvey, he had autism. Her story was horrifying. I can't imagine Harvey being sectioned and put in a room on his own. He wouldn't cope. He would kick off and start headbutting the walls. That would affect anyone really badly, never mind someone with disabilities. I was adamant that it would never happen to Harvey, but after hearing so many stories, it does happen a lot.

There are over 2,000 people with autism who are sectioned. And once you're in that system, it can take up to five years to get out, which is so scary. That's why it was so important for me to find the right college for Harvey and make sure he was around people who could cope with him.

Now, the biggest challenge for Harvey is seeing how he adapts and develops in a completely new environment with completely new people.

It's a little bit worrying, but it's definitely a good thing. I think he became too comfortable at Linden Lodge. If his teacher was off and someone else had to take over, Harvey would kick off. He becomes very set in his ways. He also knew which corridors to avoid because he knew exactly which doors would bang. His school always used to say he knows how to work the system. But that's the polite way of putting it. The word I use is crafty – *very* crafty!

But he's now in an unknown environment and they're all going to have to work it out together. I know he's going to miss school, but it's a new era for him.

Who knows what's next for Harvey. When it comes to getting a job, my mum has always been hopeful that he'll be able to. I always have to say to her, 'Calm down, Mum! Let's take it one step at a time.'

I'd really love for him to do something artistic, like illustrating his own story books. He's so talented. I want to show off his work in an art exhibition and then maybe even make a calendar out of his drawings, with half of the money going into Harvey's trust fund and the other half going to charity. Harvey has had a personal trust fund since he was younger and every time he gets a paid job, I put the money into that.

There was a young man with Down's Syndrome in America who loved colourful socks, so he went into business with his dad and designed his own range. He's made a lot of money from it, while also raising awareness of his disability, which is so inspiring. Maybe Harvey could do something like that.

Or maybe he'll do something that involves music. I think whatever he ends up doing, it will definitely be creative. There are places that do employ people like Harvey, but the only problem with Harvey is that something could suddenly upset him, like a door banging. So if that happened, he'd kick off in the middle of the workplace, which isn't ideal.

Luckily, I can help him earn money by going down other avenues. I know that he's very fortunate that he's able to do that. Harvey doesn't even realise, but he helps raise so much awareness for people with disabilities. He's proof that you can still do things and you're not limited just because you're disabled. The world really is his oyster, but at the moment, my focus is on him succeeding at college.

In these next six years, he might learn something new while he's there and he might want to do something else.

I'm positive about the future. Of course the future is unpredictable – it is for everyone. But right now, I know that Harvey is in a place where he's going to thrive. Like any mum, all I want is for my son to be happy. I couldn't be prouder of what he's achieved.

At the beginning of the book, I said I wanted to give Harvey a voice. I hope you've been able to hear his voice loud and clear. If I can do anything to raise awareness about disabilities, I will. I want to prove that having disabilities shouldn't hold you back – and I hope by telling our story we've done that.

As I write this now, Harvey has been at National Star for almost a month and I've already seen a huge change in him.

Sitting on FaceTime, I'm filled with so much pride to see him excelling in his environment. Harvey may not be with me physically, but our bond is way stronger than the distance between us. He tells me about his day and how much fun he's having. And then we finish the call the same way we always do.

'I love you.'

'I love you too, Mummy.'

'Forever?'

'Forever.'